WOODLAND WALKS
in Central England

Webb&Bower
OS Ordnance Survey

WOODLAND WALKS
in Central England
Gerald Wilkinson

First published in Great Britain in 1986 by
Webb & Bower (Publishers) Limited,
9 Colleton Crescent, Exeter, Devon EX2 4BY, and
Ordnance Survey,
Romsey Road, Maybush, Southampton So9 4 DH
in association with
Michael Joseph Limited,
44 Bedford Square, London WC1B 3DU

Designed by Peter Wrigley

Production by Nick Facer

British Library Cataloguing in Publication Data

Wilkinson, Gerald
    The Ordnance Survey woodland walks in
    South-East England.
    1. Forests and forestry—England—South East
    2. South-East (England)—Description and travel
    —Guide-books
    I. Title
    914.22′04858   DA670.S63

    ISBN 0–86350–056–0

Typeset in Great Britain by Keyspools Limited, Golborne, Lancashire
Printed and bound in Great Britain by Hazell Watson and Viney Limited,
Member of the BPCC Group, Aylesbury, Bucks

TITLE PAGE
Cannock Chase

Contents

Introduction

If you were to hover about a mile above Edge Hill near Banbury and look west, north and east over the ground of this volume, a splendid panorama of England would be spread before you: the old kingdoms of Mercia and East Anglia. Yet the 180-mile-wide, 90-mile-deep area is a plain, and contains comparatively little of our best known scenery, which tends to be hilly if not mountainous. At the perimeter are several 'Edges': the Malvern Hills, the Clee Hills, Wenlock Edge and The Wrekin are grouped at the left. The Wrekin and Wenlock Edge are wooded, but the others are ridge walks, as remarkable for their views of the Welsh hills beyond as for anything else.

Still focusing on the far horizons, the country to the right of Wales and beyond is flat, and you might glimpse the modest heights of the Delamere Forest beyond the small ridge of Peckforton in the Cheshire Plain. Beyond these is the gleam of the Mersey with the dim smudges of South Lancashire a hundred miles away.

Directly northwards the fair green hills of the White Peak form a considerable upland rising to a real mountain, over 2000 feet, in Kinder Scout – other dark peaks beyond. We may distinguish Axe Edge just to the left of Kinder, part of the gritstone fringe of the White Peak's limestone. We can see right up the Derwent Valley, beyond Matlock, towards the eastern edge of the Millstone Grit. To the left and right of the Peak District are Manchester and Sheffield. Only a little to the right of Matlock, whose moors are dark with new conifers, are the several large green patches of Sherwood Forest, a little misted by Derby and Nottingham. Then the Trent, turning northwards, is aligned to our vision, with the Lincoln Edge a marvellously straight line beside it. This Edge, once beyond Lincoln, merely sinks to the Humber. To the right of Lincoln the Wolds can provide clean, clear views when you are in them, and they have good trees and some interesting woods. Continuing clockwise, the distant country

seems to slide imperceptibly into the Wash; there are few features, except for some high ground at Cromer, to distinguish the coastline from the grey North Sea. The land is very flat, but not without its mysteries, among them some truly ancient woods.

These are the horizons. But drawing our gaze inland (and turning now from right to left) the several large, dark patches we see are the new forests, part of the most obvious change that has been made to Britain's landscape in the present century. There are forests on the east-coast sands, and some distance inland, where 200 square miles of sandy, low ground known as Breckland lie beyond the tiny Gog Magog Hills and the (almost) treeless downs of Newmarket. Within Breckland are 70 square miles of pines – the Thetford Forest.

In the centre of our enormous view the darkest features are great towns and cities of the West Midlands. Beyond is the high ground, sandy again, of Cannock Chase: half conifer plantations and half birchwood heath, and still one of the largest woodlands in England.

The Midland Plain now spread beneath us is certainly not empty of trees. The distinct pattern of more or less geometrically enclosed fields below soon turns, as distance increases, to a more even pattern of treetops. From a distance this intricate jigsaw of fields, hedges, roads and buildings all masked by trees looks like woodland. It is tempting to think of this as the original forest, or at least its leafy skeleton, but this is quite erroneous. Oak is the commonest tree now, and may have been in the distant past, but that is the only similarity. The dominant tree of the Midlands in prehistory may well have been the alternative species of oak, *Quercus petraea*, the sessile oak that is now one of the indicators of ancient woodland, or the small-leaved lime. There is no fossil record for the central Midlands.

The Plain is fairly uneventful, except for the curious humps of the Charnwood Forest

6

north-west of Leicester. These are prominences of hard, old volcanic rock that were less eroded by the ice than was the surrounding New Red Sandstone. The Forest of Arden, enclosing Stratford and Coventry, is neither more nor less wooded than the rest of the country. Only careful investigation on the ground reveals any old woodland at all. West of Birmingham there are many sandy heights and commons, with birch and pine. Along the wide Severn Vale to the Wyre Forest is a fairly small patch of conifers, about 12 square miles, to match the great Thetford Forest in the east. Under cover of the Forestry Commission's pines and Douglas firs, however, nature continues a secret, indigenous existence. But at our present height it needs no imagination to see that the wilder country is to the west in the Welsh Borders.

Now let us suppose we could take up our unlikely position an even more unlikely 6000 years back in time. What should we see below us? Instead of the patchwork of fields, the landscape would be composed in wide, sweeping curves. The ridge immediately beneath is forested, but it looks over a lake, and much of the land beyond is submerged. The rivers are very wide – nothing but water is to be seen between the Cotswolds to our left and the Malvern ridge – and there are many large, shallow lakes in the Midland Plain. Higher ground is covered by trees: pine, birch and hazel form large woods into which oaks, elms and limes are spreading – or ash and maple on more lime-rich soil. Wide banks of alder carr in low ground are little defined at this height, but the lighter greens of willows and the grey of sea buckthorn broadly outline the sheets of water. Wide marshy banks carry reed beds and enormous patches of yellow water-lilies. Occasional rocks are yellow with stonecrop, saxifrage, mountain avens and some alpine flowers now unfamiliar. Abundant plants of the meltwaters are marsh cinquefoil, bogbean, *Alisma* (water-plantain) and beak-sedge. On recently dried-out land are acres of herbaceous lily and devil's-bit scabious.

The rising ground of what is now Birmingham is densely forested and similar forests occupy the Northampton Uplands

slightly to our right. Mountains on the northern and western perimeters of our view are snow-covered and have the remains of glaciers still in their valleys. The shoreline to the north-east is not visible: only a sandy, grassy, plain, dark in places with large pinewoods interspersed with miles of sweetgale, stretches out into the delta of the Rhine. A forest fire clouds the air over the pines: clearings are being made by our first farmers. The Thames, miles wide, and a confluence of streams draining the east Midlands, flow north-east to join the Rhine. Far beyond are the North Sea deeps, full of icebergs from the Scandinavian ice cliffs.

It is a land in the process of drying out, clean, new and rich in the basic chemistry of the rocks. The forest of northern Europe slowly advances across the land in a climate rapidly improving to become warmer than our own, but no drier, and very favourable to deciduous trees. There are grazing animals to eat the tree seedlings, but they have their predators, now extinct. It is a virgin land, inhabited by families living in forest clearings, in the huts of lake dwellings, or in the sandstone caves. But the clearing process has begun – and of the subtle modification of the native forest (for even small clearings admit berry-bearing shrubs and trees).

As we turn the clock forward again we see that the forest remains and even enlarges as the wetlands disappear, then is gradually cleared century by century as more and more people demand food from the land: only kings may hunt the deer. Perhaps the trees seem to creep back a little at times, over fields temporarily abandoned to scrub. The patterns of the woods change as coppices are maintained or parks enclosed. Open fields gradually disappear and many hedges are planted, where trees again grow to fill the distances and shade the foreground. In the process, the tree cover has changed its 'skin' several times, and it is surprising that any sort of continuity can be traced.

But more intriguing than these rapid views of history, would be to continue in time, for another thousand years, to about AD 3000. Then I hope we shall see a much simplified, more open or at least less rigidly compartmented country than the one we are familiar with. Wide grasslands and large woodlands express the geography of the land, instead of the present close-knit texture where the various interests compete with each other over every square foot, and nature hides for safety. Old scars and industrial mess are long ago healed over and cleared away, and the natural landscape has once again taken over – albeit on altered soils and drainage. By this time we have solved the problems of housing and feeding a large population by other means than the continual destruction of natural resources. Travel no longer depends on the proliferation of 'spaghetti junctions' and land-consuming tarmac, nor on a noisy invasion of the sky. All is accomplished under the ground. The land is for walking on.

The Forest of Arden has returned, as have other ancient forests, and the West Midlands, thanks to its conservation-minded administration long ago in the 2000s, is largely green, a setting for some remarkable museums. To the west we notice a feature that can be identified: the Big Trees of Queen's Wood are now in middle age, the now square tops easily visible 50 miles away against the blue of the Welsh mountains. The wilderness of Wales is little changed over the centuries, for no one wanted to lose all the open moors – but the Welsh forests are no longer dedicated to producing softwoods and the range of habitat is immensely increased.

There is, inevitably, a great deal of control and active conservation in the countryside of 3000, but it is so completely informed and so subtly carried out that everywhere nature seems to be simply taking her own course.

To the east and north-east, the coastline has again become unrecognizable. Vast stretches of the Wash and the shallower parts of the North Sea are now dry, and very fertile. This is the food production zone, as refreshing to look at, with its landscaping of shelter-belts and bird sanctuary woodlands and meres, as the largely recreational heart of England. All the hard work of the country, apart from this essential eastern agriculture, goes on underground – and no one needs to spend much time working.

A thousand years of advanced technology has had its problems, but communication has not been one of them. War and famine are now ruled out. The surface of the earth is now free to return, with guidance, to its natural state. The climate in the North temperate zone is poor, but the people are not at its mercy and look forward with confidence to the re-advance of the ice. The period of history between the Middle Ages and the twentieth century is seen as an awkward transitional stage, a sad and dangerous time only relieved by its aspiring and highly individual art, music and literature and its pioneering sciences. The people struggled in the mires of their own creating, and dreamed of a Utopian future without ever really believing in it.

But now it is time to come down to earth and examine the thin traces of our woodland heritage. The continuity is almost lost, and if our native vegetation with most of its associated fauna is to survive into the next millennium we shall need to know how it works and what it is made of. Woodland walks are innocent and enjoyable exercises, but you can, if you are so inclined, take them very seriously.

Key

The book is divided into sections which follow on numerically from west to east and south to north of the region. At the beginning of each section the relevant Ordnance Survey Landranger sheet numbers are listed. Each entry is headed with factual information in the form below:

a   b   c

Burrator Forest *568 694,* ♀ ✹, *1000 acres, paths and a forest road, WA*

d   e

a Ordnance Survey National Grid
  reference – usually of the nearest car park
b Type of woodland: ♀ deciduous
  ✦ coniferous ✹ marsh
c Size of wooded area
d Type of walk
e Owner of site

How to find a grid reference

The reference for Burrator Forest is *568 694*

56 – Can be found in the top and bottom margins of the relevant map sheet (identified at the start of each book section). It is the reference number for one of the grid lines running north/south on the map.
69 – Can be found in the left and right hand margins of the relevant map sheet. It is the reference number for one of the grid lines running east/west on the map.

These numbers locate the bottom left hand corner of the kilometre grid square in which the car park for Burrator Forest appears. The remaining figures of the reference (*568 694*) pinpoint the feature within the grid square to the nearest 100 metres as shown in the diagram below.

The following abbreviations are used:
AONB Area of outstanding natural beauty
CNT   *County Naturalists' Trust*
CP   Country Park
FC   Forestry Commission
FNR   Forest Nature Reserve
fp   footpath
GLC   Greater London Council
LA   Local Authority
LNR   Local Nature Reserve
MAFF Ministry of Agriculture Fisheries and
          Food
NC   Nature Conservancy
NNR   National Nature Reserve
NT   National Trust
NTS   National Trust for Scotland
pf   private forestry
SSSI Site of Special Scientific Interest
SWT   Scottish Wildlife Trust
WA   Water Authority
WT   Woodland Trust

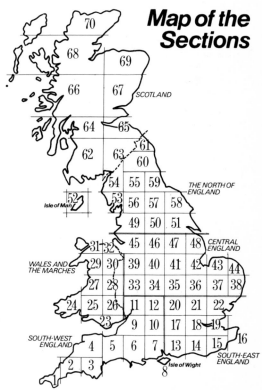

Map of the Sections

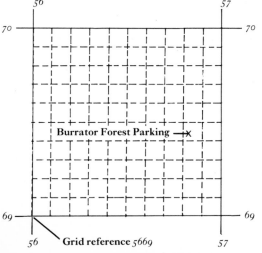

Grid reference *5669*

The dotted lines within the square do not appear on the face of the map

1:316,800 maps

RELIEF

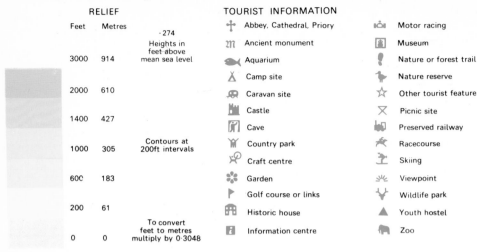

Feet	Metres	
		·274
		Heights in feet above mean sea level
3000	914	
2000	610	
1400	427	
1000	305	Contours at 200ft intervals
600	183	
200	61	
0	0	To convert feet to metres multiply by 0·3048

TOURIST INFORMATION

- ☩ Abbey, Cathedral, Priory
- ₥ Ancient monument
- 🐟 Aquarium
- ⋏ Camp site
- 🚐 Caravan site
- 🏰 Castle
- Cave
- Country park
- Craft centre
- ✿ Garden
- ⚑ Golf course or links
- 🏚 Historic house
- Information centre
- Motor racing
- Museum
- Nature or forest trail
- Nature reserve
- ☆ Other tourist feature
- ✕ Picnic site
- Preserved railway
- Racecourse
- Skiing
- Viewpoint
- Wildlife park
- ▲ Youth hostel
- Zoo

ROADS Not necessarily rights of way

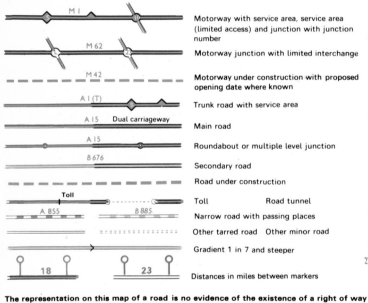

Motorway with service area, service area (limited access) and junction with junction number

Motorway junction with limited interchange

Motorway under construction with proposed opening date where known

Trunk road with service area

Main road

Roundabout or multiple level junction

Secondary road

Road under construction

Toll   Road tunnel

Narrow road with passing places

Other tarred road   Other minor road

Gradient 1 in 7 and steeper

Distances in miles between markers

The representation on this map of a road is no evidence of the existence of a right of way

GENERAL FEATURES

- Buildings
- Wood
- Lighthouse (in use)
- Lighthouse (disused)
- ⚵ Windmill
- Radio or TV mast
- Youth hostel
- ⊕ Civil aerodrome { with Customs facilities
- ✚ { without Customs facilities
- Ⓗ Heliport
- ℂ Public telephone
- Motoring organisation telephone

ANTIQUITIES

- ✳ Native fortress
- 𝔠𝔞𝔰𝔱𝔩𝔢 · Other antiquities
- ⚔ Site of battle (with date)
- ---- Roman road (course of)
- CANOVIUM · Roman antiquity
- ₥ Ancient Monuments and Historic Buildings in the care of the Secretaries of State for the Environment, for Scotland and for Wales and that are open to the public.

WATER FEATURES

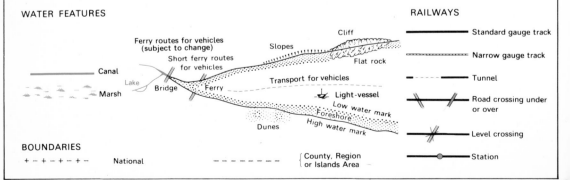

- Canal
- Lake
- Marsh
- Ferry routes for vehicles (subject to change)
- Short ferry routes for vehicles
- Bridge
- Ferry
- Cliff
- Slopes
- Flat rock
- Transport for vehicles
- Light-vessel
- Low water mark
- Foreshore
- High water mark
- Dunes

RAILWAYS

- Standard gauge track
- Narrow gauge track
- Tunnel
- Road crossing under or over
- Level crossing
- Station

BOUNDARIES

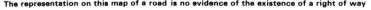

- + - + - + - + - National
- — — — — — { County, Region or Islands Area

1:50,000 maps

ROADS AND PATHS Not necessarily rights of way

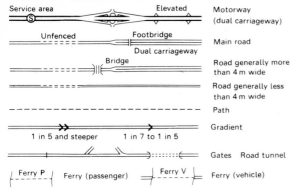

Service area — Elevated — Motorway (dual carriageway)

Unfenced — Footbridge — Main road

Dual carriageway

Bridge — Road generally more than 4 m wide

Road generally less than 4 m wide

Path

Gradient

1 in 5 and steeper   1 in 7 to 1 in 5

Gates   Road tunnel

Ferry P   Ferry (passenger)   Ferry V   Ferry (vehicle)

PUBLIC RIGHTS OF WAY (Not applicable to Scotland)

Public rights of way indicated by these symbols have been
derived from Definitive Maps as amended by later enactments
or instruments held by Ordnance Survey on and are shown subject
to the limitations imposed by the scale of mapping

**The representation on this map of any other road, track or
path is no evidence of the existence of a right of way**

TOURIST INFORMATION

- **i** Information centre
- **P** Parking
- **P**
- ✗ Picnic site
- ✆ Telephone, public/motoring organisation
- ⌐ Golf course or links
- **PC** Public convenience (in rural areas)
- ☀ Viewpoint

WATER FEATURES

Marsh or salting   Slopes   Cliff   High water mark

Towpath   Lock   Flat rock   Low water mark

Aqueduct   Canal   Ford   Lighthouse (in use)

Weir   Sand

Lake   Normal tidal limit   Dunes   Beacon

Bridge

Footpath   Lighthouse (disused)   Shingle

Mud   Mud

Canal (dry)

BOUNDARIES

— + — + — National

— o — o — o — London Borough

— · — · — · — County, Region or Islands Area

— + — + — + — District

ANTIQUITIES

VILLA Roman   ⚔ Battlefield (with date)   + Position of antiquity which cannot be drawn to scale

Castle Non-Roman   ☆ Tumulus

The revision date of archaeological information varies over the sheet

RAILWAYS

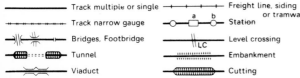

Track multiple or single   Freight line, siding or tramway

Track narrow gauge   Station

Bridges, Footbridge   Level crossing

Tunnel   Embankment

Viaduct   Cutting

GENERAL FEATURES

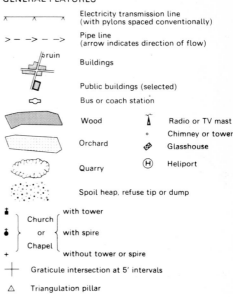

Electricity transmission line (with pylons spaced conventionally)

Pipe line (arrow indicates direction of flow)

Buildings

Public buildings (selected)

Bus or coach station

Wood

Orchard

Quarry

Spoil heap, refuse tip or dump

Church or Chapel { with tower / with spire / without tower or spire }

Graticule intersection at 5' intervals

△ Triangulation pillar

Windmill with or without sails

- ⊺ Radio or TV mast
- ○ Chimney or tower
- ⚲ Glasshouse
- Ⓗ Heliport
- Windpump

HEIGHTS

·144   Heights are to the nearest metre above mean sea level

Heights shown close to a triangulation pillar refer to the station
height at ground level and not necessarily to the summit.

ABBREVIATIONS

P	Post office
PH	Public house
MS	Milestone
MP	Milepost
CH	Clubhouse
PC	Public convenience (in rural areas)
TH	Town Hall, Guildhall or equivalent
CG	Coastguard

HOW TO GIVE A GRID REFERENCE (BRITISH NATIONAL GRID)

100 000 Metre GRID SQUARE IDENTIFICATION

SN   SO   2 00

SS   ST

3 00

IGNORE the SMALLER figures of any grid number: these are for finding the full coordinates. Use ONLY the LARGER figure of the grid number.

EXAMPLE: 2**69**000m

TO GIVE A GRID REFERENCE TO NEAREST 100 METRES

SAMPLE POINT: The Talbots

1. Read letters identifying 100 000 metre square in which the point lies.   ST

2. FIRST QUOTE EASTINGS Locate first VERTICAL grid line to LEFT of point and read LARGE figures labelling the line either in the top or bottom margin or on the line itself. Estimate tenths from grid line to point.   05   7

3. AND THEN QUOTE NORTHINGS Locate first HORIZONTAL grid line BELOW point and read LARGE figures labelling the line either in the left or right margin or on the line itself. Estimate tenths from grid line to point.   70   7

SAMPLE REFERENCE   ST 057 707

For local referencing grid letters may be omitted.

30	39	40
28	**33**	34
26	11	12

CENTRAL ENGLAND
Wyre and West of Birmingham

Landranger sheets 137, 138, 149

Queenswood CP, *Dinmore Hill*
506 515, ♀ ♣, 170 acres, easy walking, many options, LA
The A49 from Hereford to Leominster curves up the hill, which is Old Red Sandstone. The parking place is on the left going north, with a café, and a shop open between April and September. An unmetalled road penetrates the wood just beyond the parking ground, which is rather exposed and noisy. Midland buses pass every two hours, some from Birmingham.

The wood really did belong to the Queen, until it was sold in the eighteenth century. All the fine oaks and beeches were cut down in World War I and the land left to regenerate into wilderness. The Council for the Preservation of Rural England saved it from being built upon; it was bought by Herefordshire County with the proceeds of a memorial fund to King George V's Silver Jubilee, and dedicated to the public 'for all time'.

Half is forestry, oak and other native trees, and is a nature reserve. The centre plateau contains a beautifully planned arboretum of 400 varieties of tree – probably over 200 species. All are grouped and arranged as open woodland, with blocks of conifers and stands of native oak intervening. Infant *Sequoiadendron* and others, planted out, seem to suggest a plan

in the grand manner to be realized in the next century. Then, floating up from Hereford by hovercraft, you will see Queenswood crowned with a ring of the largest trees in the world.

Several fine Japanese cherries were spectacular in late March. All the trees have numbered posts and a catalogue can be bought at the café. Numbering is a sensible system, because people steal name-plates – and the catalogue provides a portable memorandum; it includes, also, lists of wild flowers and birds.

Queenswood is an excellent Country Park, with inspired management and a beautiful situation 600 feet above the surrounding countryside; it is only marred by the noise of lorries grinding up the A49.

On the A44, 2 miles east of Bromyard, is the large **Brockhampton** estate of the National Trust, with woodland walks: *693 543*.

WENLOCK EDGE

The Edge is characteristically wooded, there not being much else to do with it, but most of the woodland is a very steep, narrow strip of thicket. Whatever troubled the wood in Housman's time has resulted in a number of car parks in a place where there is not room for them, and an even greater number of large, ugly concrete litter bins. The National Trust part begins where the cement works finish, on the B4371 a mile or two south-west of Much Wenlock, and there are ways into the escarpment wood. Avoiding all this, you can drive on to Rushbury and take the road past the church and over the hill into Hope Dale; there is space to park in a muddy lane which leads promisingly off westwards, at the map reference given below: it is signposted Bridleway. This is north of Upper Millichope.

A Hope Dale Walk *518 898, ♀ ♣,*
2½ hours, very muddy (clay), fps
The bridleway is churned by farm tractors but the voices of sheep in the upland air will charm

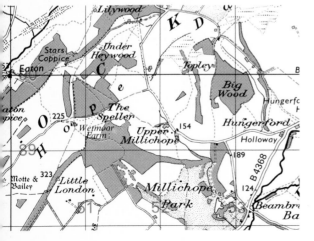

Prunus incisa in April,
Queenswood

you, and the light beckons beyond a wooded hill, a lesser Edge. The way leads through very straight poplars, contrasting with crooked old oaks – some are durmast oaks. Then at the gate, where Sitka spruce forestry begins on the right, you can choose to cross the pasture, left, or follow the lane to the farm, according to whether you wish to go clockwise or anti-, I will assume the latter. The farm is lovely, all patches of corrugated iron, with an open paddock full of geese and ducks, and, in March, expectant ewes loudly demanding more to eat. A hollow lane leads uphill beyond the farm; you will then see a small gate into the

Forestry and natural vegetation in Hope Dale

wood at the top of the pasture. The view of Wales is terrific. The wood, once a coppice, no doubt to supply fuel to the farm, is now quite neglected, with dog's mercury in the deeply engraved path. With some difficulty you can reach the plateau, which has a most impressive group of old Scots pines and larches over soft green grass – a perfect picnic place on a warm day.

Turning back, the ridge passes around a healthy stand of Corsican pine, which makes a plain, dark frame for the pretty hills beyond. When you reach the larchwood beyond the iron railings of Millichope Park, turn downhill, sharp left, to return to the farm. An old birchwood offers another contrast with the geometry of modern forestry. Leaving the farm on your left, a gate leads into the pasture with its picturesque durmast oaks, one of which has a yew growing out of its top, and back to the poplar patch.

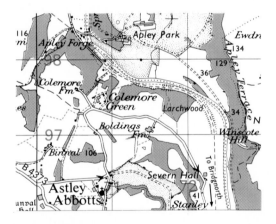

NEAR BRIDGNORTH

A Severn Valley Walk *718 970*, ♀ , *about 2m, easy*
Go north out of Bridgnorth on the B4373 for ½ mile, then turn right at the first opportunity, down Stanley Lane. Small factories and a golf club give a misleading impression of what turns out to be a pleasant rural lane leading only to farms and a tiny hamlet, Colemore Green. A small area of tarmac marks a parking place, probably made for fishermen, and here

you can strike off by a well-trodden bridleway through a larchwood, to join a dirt road on the track of an old railway. The steep terraces and the riverside are wooded, but more interesting for their shapes than for their trees. The area is rich in wild flowers.

A lovely white suspension bridge at the now converted railway station of Linley was built in 1909 and carries a cast-iron inscription by which Mr Foster, presumably of Apley Park, across the water, allowed no one but his estate workers to use the bridge without permisssion. Apart from the conifers of the estate plantation the riverside woods are of poplar – the dullest hybrid black, but a good crop.

Long-distance walkers can continue to Coalport and to Iron-Bridge, but to regain your car retreat to a farm track which leaves the valley by a small cottage, passing an ancient, gnarled alder, to Colemore Farm and back by the road.

Badger Dingle *766 995*, ♀ (♠), *1m or less*
The only reasonable place to park is by the little cemetery shelter in Badger: the path leads straight down to this heavily wooded stream valley. There is a footpath along the north bank, but the upper part of the stream is choked with dead elms and is a jungle. The wood is extraordinary, a ruined mixture of Victorian planting over what must have been originally a natural beauty-spot. The Red Sandstone miniature terraces, boldly carved by the ancient stream, are surmounted by great knotted roots of oaks and yews. Now it may be a great oak or beech, or a *Sequoiadendron* which next crashes across the stream, as many have done already.

Nothing but the oaks, which are large, can be accepted as original vegetation, so much was planted; and there was even a belvedere, now ruined, from which to survey the fairy dell. *Mahonia* spreads unattractively with fierce yellow flowers in early spring. There are patches of butcher's broom, and in the streamside mud a splendid array of butterbur against the background of mossy, fallen trunks. Both these plants could be native but equally could have been planted; even butterbur has its use for early bee food. One of the yews is the Irish (fastigiate) cultivar gone shapeless, the others look native.

Further upstream the rocks are covered with vivid green moss, and masses of yellow-green spurge. Willows spread over and dead elm trunks criss-cross the stream. There is a giant hybrid poplar, and still there are good oaks: but the path becomes impossible.

Local farmers have put up 'private' notices here and there, probably to protect the fishing, and the edges of the wood are used to dump rubbish.

WEST OF BIRMINGHAM

Highgate Common CP *836 901*, ♀ ♠ , *350 acres, easy, many paths, LA*
This is a Black Country common on black sand with dark stands of pine and a splendid wide sweep of heather and birch, all strangely tinged with the colour of the soil. Even the silver birches have a distinctly darkling gleam as if drawn in Indian ink. A no-go area in the middle, ringed with thicker birchwood,

contains a mysterious black wooden shed with a green door. The central car park has an ice-cream van on bank holidays: on an ordinary day you could have the place almost to yourself.

The Common was the subject of intricate legal arguments over ownership: the Lord of the Manor claiming it was his freehold; the Forestry Commission acquiring a lease to plant the usual pole crop, and the County Council opposing this, then buying the land for us – many thanks!

Kinver Edge *837 836*, ♀ ♠ , *400 acres, ridge walk, easy but a stiff climb, NT*
Kingsford CP *823 823*, ♀ ♠ , *trails, including a disabled trail, CC*
The ridge of Kinver Edge runs south-south-west from Kinver's west side to a high central point, with birch woodland broadening down to the wider Country Park which is in largely conifer plantation. I have given the map reference of the Country Park: you may choose the better of the two areas which I think is to

Highgate Common, a darker-than-usual birch heath

the north: here, there are many parking places. The Country Park has all the amenities; a waymarked walk, a nature trail with explanatory notices, a disabled trail, a camping site, and a horse route; and 160 acres of forestry conifers if you want to shut out the world. But the Edge is something else; an experience of superb birchwoods sweeping up to the cliff, where oaks and thorns cling, with gorse to catch you if you fall. The wide path on the top gives views of what looks like most of the Midlands, smooth green fields and farms intervening. At the Kinver end, perched over the town, is Holy Austin Rock, site of the last troglodyte dwelling in Britain, vacated only in the fifties and with gas still laid on. The pink

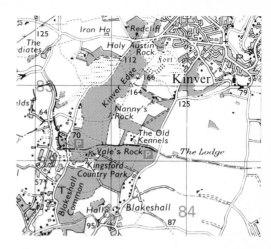

On Kinver Edge

sandstone was carved into rooms with doors and windows, a Scots pine growing out of the rocks in the front garden. The caves, believed to have been occupied more or less continuously since the Iron Age, are now covered in deeply incised graffiti. The rich colour and irregular lines imposed by the strata (impossible to imagine the river bed that formed them) give the inscriptions an unmistakable Egyptian hieroglyphic character. How strongly a wall of soft rock appeals to the monumental inscriber in all of us, particularly one REBECCA who must have spent the day on the job. But we stray from the woods.

Wyre Forest *762 779,* ♀ ♠ *, at least 6000 acres, 2 picnic sites with various forest walks, FC*
Wyre was originally home to the Weogorena Tribe. The Romans named Worcester VVIOGORNA CEASTRE and Wyre stuck for the forest area, then almost the whole county including part of Shropshire as well. Later, the Crown held some rights, but the locals tried to contain the deer with a 4-mile fence. Tall trees were cut to make charcoal for the iron industry. Coppicing and itinerant charcoal burning continued well into this century, and most of the forest woods are either commons or

The Wyre Forest – north-western edges

named coppices. Bewdley's Town Coppice is at least 300 acres. Industry, demanding a renewable source of fuel, preserved the coppices, which also supplied the valuable oak bark for tanning. Not only for harness and clothing, leather was essential for bellows, even more so when coke began to fire the furnaces in the nineteenth century. It was left to the Forestry Commission to destroy most of this centuries-old heritage of woodland.

The major portion of the forest is now contained between the B4194 and A4117 running west from Bewdley. The Forestry Commission maintains two parking areas with picnic places and shortish walks. The map

Wyre Forest floor: beneath the scion of the wild sorb tree, and, BELOW, bilbery and moss-covered remains of oak coppice

reference above is for the quieter place, Hawkbatch, on the B4194. It is a lovely spot and gives access to the Severn Valley side and **Seckley Wood**, *765 786*, home of some ancient beeches. At the main car park on the A road, *751 742*, the longest of three walks from the Visitors' Centre takes you right into the forest over Dowles Brook. Knowles Coppice and Fred Dale, together 72 acres, are nature reserves in the valley, served by footpaths along the brook. Coppices have grown up into oak forest. Knowles Mill by the brook is National Trust property with an old orchard. Somewhere in the forest grew the famous, lonely Whitty Pear, recorded as *Sorbus pyriformis* in the seventeenth century, the only wild individual of the species in Britain (the tree is native as far north as Brittany). That old tree was vandalized in the nineteenth century but its seedlings were used to replace it. Now a neat label identifies the 'sorb tree' – it is *Sorbus domestica*, and all the mystery is gone, along with the oaks removed by the Forestry Commission.

Walking into the forest from the west, say at Sturt Common, *725 774*, can give some idea of the older countryside where farms, forest and heath interpenetrate. Half a square mile of the Longdon and Withybed woods north of Dowles Brook are protected by covenant to the National Trust, and we may hope that all the forest is not lost to the Douglas fir and the pines, though the view from rising ground to the west seems to say otherwise. The best walk is probably along the Dowles Brook, left from the B4194, one mile north-west of Bewdley.

A comprehensive and splendidly illustrated book on the Wyre Forest is N. E. Hickin's *Natural History of an English Forest*, 1971. It deals largely with herbaceous plants and with animals, amongst which on site I noticed, short-sightedly, tutsan and wood ants – the latter you can hardly miss.

Worcester has an oakwood, **Nunnery Wood**, *875 545*, 55 acres, only a mile from the city centre on the A422 behind County Hall and owned by the County Council, containing ash and wild service, with helleborine, cow wheat, tormentil and hairy rush.

Only 12 miles south-west of the centre of Birmingham the **Clent Hills** have a Country Park, *927 799*. The common of 166 acres and Walton Hill Common, 86 acres, were purchased by the county from the Lord of the Manor, Lord Cobham. Lords of Manors own little but the soil of a common, and have many responsibilities. The County Council wanted Lord Cobham to continue his lordship of the Manor, against his inclination. A Royal Commission had to sit. Eventually, 362 acres were given to the National Trust, and with many local authorities assisting, Lord Cobham was allowed to retire. The commons are surrounded by close-packed country residences.

Shrawley Wood, on the Severn at *805 663*, is described as an oakwood containing the greatest remaining concentration of the native small-leaved lime. Lime was the dominant tree in this area according to the fossil record from gravel dated 7500 to 2500 years ago. There is nothing in Shrawley Wood to suggest a continuous history except for a few old coppiced stools. The effect, on a dull day, was slightly depressing, but I am always too influenced by the weather. The oaks are at the edges. Two signed footpaths eastwards leave the B4196 south of Stourport near two pubs. As there is nowhere special to park a car I have given a map reference only for the centre of the woodland.

Autumn leaves in Shrawley Wood

Shrawley church is about a mile south of the wood. It is very pretty, pink and lopsided, and flanked by two fine large trees: a hornbeam and a sweet chestnut.

Chaddesley Woods, *914 736*, oak and conifer, attempt to show that conservation and commercial forestry are compatible: a National Nature Reserve too, with species associated with ancient woodland, including the wild service tree and the so-called Midland hawthorn.

Waseley Hills Country Park, *979 768*, contains **Sedgbourne Coppice**, and scrubland.

Pepper Wood, *940 750*, 134 acres just 5 miles north-west of Bromsgrove, is a valuable acquisition of the Woodland Trust, particularly as it is so close to the great conurbation. It is a wet, overgrown coppice-with-standards which the Trust is to manage and whose traditional products will be used.

Piper's Hill Common, *957 648*, astride the B4091 north of Hanbury, is wooded and carefully controlled by the Lord of the Manor. It is a Site of Special Scientific Interest.

The Avoncroft Museum, *952 684*, Stoke Heath, rescues timber buildings. On site, among others, is a windmill in working order and a very interesting cruck barn, the cruck of black poplar. In appearance as soft as balsa wood, the great knotty beams have held the structure for nearly four centuries. The native black poplar was once common in the Midland farmlands and the largest tree available – hence its use for building. There are now only 2000 individuals left in the whole country.

Himley Plantation, Wombourne
870 914, ♀ ♣, *59 acres, WT*
This wood (off the B4176) was saved for us by the Woodland Trust and is part of an old estate. Rhododendron is present, with mature oak, beech and pine. A disused railway managed as a Country Park penetrates the wood and goes off south-east.

Birmingham and Warwickshire

Landranger sheets 139, 140, 150

THE FOREST OF ARDEN

> *Rosalind*: Well, this is the Forest of Arden!
> *Touchstone*: Ay, now I am in Arden, the
> more fool I! When I was at home I was in a
> better place...
>
> *As You Like It*

Rugged, shapely oaks remain, though not in
the forest glades of Shakespeare's time.
Charcoal burning for industry reduced the
forest to coppice; then, as coke and coal
became the main fuels, farming took over all
the land to supply the ever-growing
population. Orchards in the south, by the
Avon, have spread fruit trees into the hedges,
which can be of pure damson in places. Old
plums are distinctive hedgerow trees, as
frequent as poplars which are planted for
shelter. Great elms there were – it was the
'Warwickshire weed' – but all are now dead.
Still the oaks persist, but not in the woods.

Oversley Wood, Alcester *112 570*, ♀ ♣,
1½m around, FC

There is supposed to be a trail, but the marks
are lost. A right of way leads into the wood
from Primrose Hill, Oversley Green – you
have to park in the village. A stout border of
blackthorn has been cleared, but you have to
hop over barbed wire to get on to the forest
road. There is maple, birch, hazel, cherry,
rowan, sallow, holly and even a bit of oak in
places, but you look out of the wood to older
oaks. Inside are solid blocks of Corsican pine,
hemlock, larch: but the foresters have left wide
margins, birch-dominated at present. The
intention was to replace the hardwoods
eventually, or so said H. L. Edlin of the
Forestry Commission in 1958.

The proper entrance is at the north-east
corner from the A422 (Alcester to Stratford).

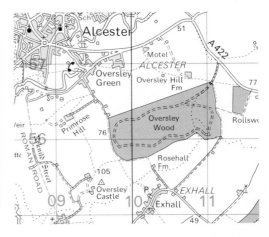

Kenilworth Castle, and an oak tree

Here you have to park in a lay-by. Do visit the wood if you can, to help convince the foresters that there is some public interest in this rather isolated piece of the Forest of Arden.

Hay Wood *207 706*, ♀ ♠ , *picnic place, FC*
Hard to find unless you know it, here is a

woodland corner with beautifully rural surroundings. The foresters have left only a small corner to walk in, and even here have planted hemlocks amongst the native trees. Some oak-ash-holly character survives. You can walk down the quiet lane to Baddesley Clinton old church.

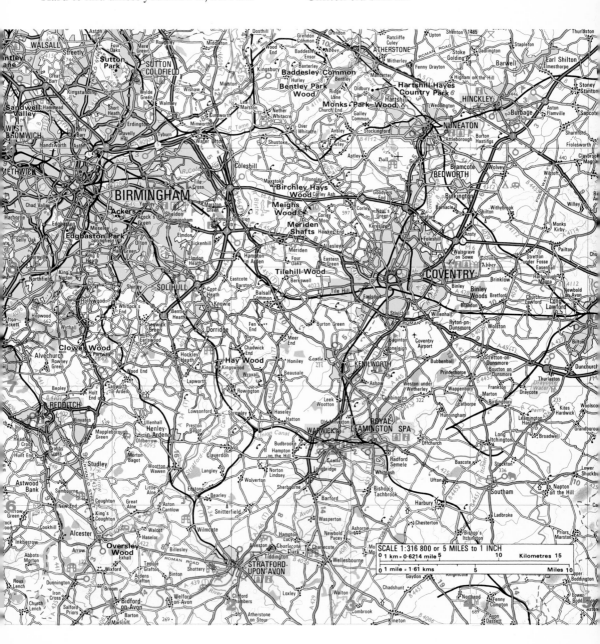

The National Trust Packwood House, timber framed, *171 722*, has, besides a famous set-piece of topiary, 113 acres of park and woodland, and is well signposted 2 miles west of the wood. But there is no right of way through the park when the garden is closed during the winter. A 'Leisure Drive' through wooded lanes may be a substitute for a walk.

Packwood House. The topiary garden beyond a mighty oak.

Meriden Shafts, *near Eaves Green,* **Meighs Wood** and **Birchley Hays Wood,** *near Hollyberry End: all around 257 837, all FC*

These coniferized corpses of old woods are non-starters for walking in, but there is a wide grassy verge to park on at the map reference, and we have marked the footpaths, hoping that you will do the exploring. Meriden Shafts is actually closed, the Forestry Commission having let the sporting rights, but this need not be permanent. How could I resist a name like that? Meriden is supposed to be the centre of England – the name probably means 'cherry wood': Shafts, a coppice – for arrow-shafts? The 'Woodmen of Arden', eighty-one crack archers, have their headquarters here. But I have to admit that 'shafts' could indicate old mine-workings.

Packington Park, to the north-west, is a 700-acre deer park. It is private, but leafy lanes to the east of the park are quiet. Before the gates are closed in the evening and guard dogs begin to prowl, one may look in at the last of the

The lake at Packwood, with poplar hybrids

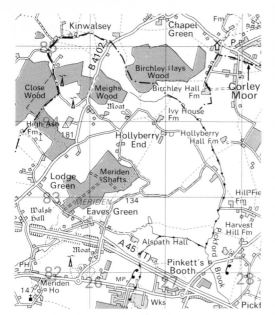

RIGHT: *Betula pendula* of horticultural origin in Packington Park contrasts with shaggy, stag-headed oaks BELOW

Chestnut and sycamore litter, Tilehill Wood

Arden oaks, enclosed by privilege and isolated by trunk roads between the cities of Birmingham and Coventry.

Hartshill Hayes Country Park, *316 947*, has woodland and adjoins Forestry Commission plantations where facilities are being developed. **Monk's Park Wood** and **Bentley Park Wood**, the largest woods in the section, are private, but there are footpaths from Birchley Heath, Ridge Lane (south from the B4116) and at Bentley Common: consult the OS map, sheet 140. **Baddesley Common**, *277 978*, has the remains of an oak coppice, next to a coal-mine – a pleasant place to stop if you are slogging up the A5: north-west of Atherstone, turn left at the Black Swan, Grendon.

Near Coventry is **Tilehill Wood**, a slightly

Baddesley Common, an attractive fragment in a tired landscape

sad survival between new housing and new factories and schools, but with some good oaks, hollies and chestnut coppice. The only place to park is on the east side, in the streets, *283 790*.

Clowes Wood and New Fallings Coppice *098 738, ♀, 150 acres, LA*

Between Birmingham and Redditch, at Tanworth-in-Arden, is Clowes Wood, a nature reserve of 77 acres, oak and beech woodland. Wood Lane, *102 743*, is one point of access, by many footpaths through New Fallings Coppice; or from Earlswood Lakes Station, across a field. Wood Lane is signposted from the north-west; to find it from the B4102 turn down at the Reservoir pub, then left *beyond* the lake. New Fallings Coppice is no longer a coppice in appearance: it has been 'promoted' to an oakwood. Alder buckthorn, and aspen in Clowes Wood (beyond the stream to the south), suggest antiquity; there trees are never planted. Clowes Wood is very varied and will repay patient exploration.

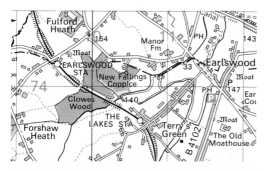

Alder buckthorn in New Fallings Coppice

The reservoir, half of it used for sailing, is a popular recreation place. There is a walk under willows along the south-east side.

There are a great number of small woods in Warwickshire, and according to statistics they contain 8000 acres of oak. Please explore, and claim your right to your woodlands. Join the County Naturalists' Trust, WARNACT. Tilehill Wood and Clowes Wood are two of close on thirty sites which the West Midlands County Council has designated as nature reserves in or very near the urban areas of Birmingham and Coventry. Not all are primarily woodland of course, but old woods and plantations of native trees are fundamental to the conservation process. Interested city-dwellers will not, I feel, despise a bog or a disused canal if there are wild flowers, birds and trees to be seen.

The concern of the West Midlands planners is threefold: to reclaim 5000 acres of derelict land; to provide much needed open spaces for one million city people; to establish semi-wild or wild nature parks, particularly where canals and rivers already admit wildlife into industrial and built-up areas. Twenty sites are currently being worked on with the help of British Trust for Conservation volunteers.

Among old-established reserves are **Edgbaston Park**, *063 832*, with a bird lake and famous botanical garden, and **Sutton Park**, *103 963*, large and popular but with some unfrequented woodland. Among new reserves on reclaimed land are **Ackers**, *103 846*, also within the City of Birmingham, and **Clayhanger**, *045 045*, and **Bentley Lane**, *985 000*, both in Walsall. These are woodland walks of the future. Walsall also has an older woodland reserve in **Merridale Cemetery**, 5 acres at *899 979*. Close to West Bromwich are the **Sandwell Valley** nature trails: *017 914*.

OVERLEAF: oaks in New Fallings Coppice

CENTRAL ENGLAND
Northamptonshire

Landranger sheets 141, 152

ROCKINGHAM FOREST

Rockingham Forest is still recognizable by a scattering of green patches on the map to the west of Oundle on the Nene and bounded by the Welland to the north-west. Place-names like Melton Mowbray and Stilton, with Laxton and Caldecott in the forest area, put one in mind of hunters leaping over hedges, and good solid food; woodland reduced to copses, coverts and apple orchards. The Forestry Commission is very much in control and occupies pieces of land not up to the standard of profitable arable farming. Occasional oaks look as if they were not up to timber standards, but confer a forest character hard to reconcile with the dull fields and hedges.

A great monument of a beech tree remains at the approach to the Forestry Commission's attractive picnic place in Wakerley Great Wood. I wonder if it was the last of the Fox Trees – awarded to keepers in Rockingham Forest for prowess in killing foxes.

Wakerley Great Wood *963 986, (♀) ♠, 100 acres, easy walks, forest trail or toughish hikes, FC*
Fine larches surround a capacious parking place and vistas of oaks and pines open out beyond. There are also unofficial grassy picnic spots along the by-road through the forest. The road is signposted Wakerley, about 7 miles north of Corby on the A43(T) to Stamford.

Ancient beech in Wakerley Great Wood

This is a cheerful-looking forest with much more to it than the regulation forest trail. On the opposite side of the A43 is Fineshade Top Lodge, the Forest Office, with Caravan Club site. Here an old railway cutting plunges into the trees to the south-west, offering another sort of walk, and Westhay Wood, a good

square mile of Commission forest, is also open to walkers; there should be something for everyone.

Short Wood, *020 912,* by permit from the NTNC, is described as a remnant of the forest and is famous for bluebells: 62 acres. **King's Wood,** *864 874,* also contains old oaks of the

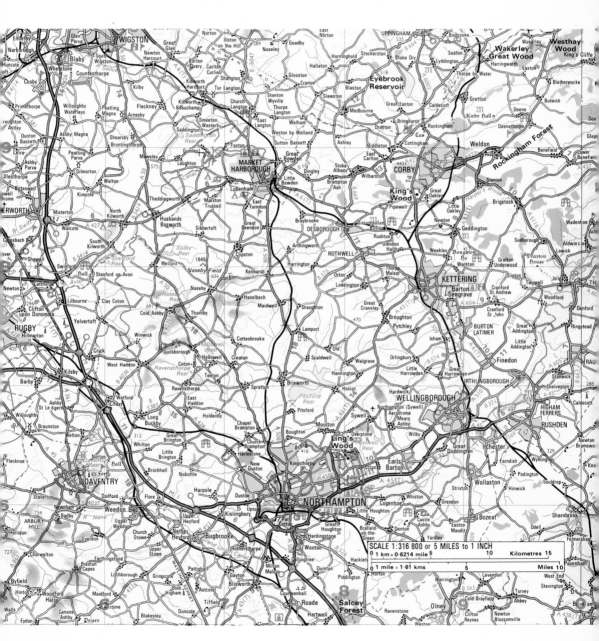

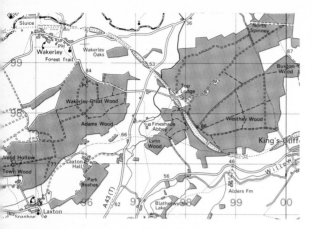

Rockingham Forest in over 100 acres. It is a nature reserve in Corby. **Lings Wood,** *803 640,* is in Northampton, a 56-acre nature reserve.

At Thrapston Gravel Pits on the Nene you can walk by fine white willows, not yet a woodland: *995 796.*

In the north east of the Rockingham Forest area near Benefield and just off our map at *003 903* is a nature reserve called Glapthorn Cow Pasture. No longer pastured it has reverted to woodland, mainly blackthorn thicket, and is known for its birds and butterflies. In such a woodland walking may be less satisfactory than sitting still.

Eyebrook Reservoir *853 964,* (♀)♣, *1½m (3m there and back), cinder road, WA*
The south-east side of the water is planted with a selection of conifers and some willows at the water's edge. (Turn off the A6003, Corby to Oakham going northwards, for Stoke Dry.) The minor road has several parking places provided for bird-watchers. A gate across the cinder road is locked to keep out vehicles and the shore is out of bounds. Walkers are expected to behave themselves and not be burdened with dogs or children. This is a peaceful place, though not to me exciting, perhaps because of the cold March wind. On a summer day the shade of these trees could be most welcome.

Pitsford Reservoir *783 707*, has a 480 acre nature reserve at the shallow end mainly for the 188 species of bird which have been seen there since 1955.

NEAR NORTHAMPTON

Salcey Forest *794 515,* ♀ ♣, *1300 acres, 2m forest trail, often muddy or wet, FC*
The M1 skirts the forest but is not too audible, being in a cutting. Approach by the B526 from Newport Pagnell, or from Northampton turn off the A508 at Wootton, and then through the village of Quinton. The nearest M1 exit is junction 15. Numerous unofficial parking places on the east–west road through the forest are provided by the concrete platforms remaining from wartime RAF occupation.

A mile of oaks is a refreshing sight on the road through the forest. The oak plantation is a Site of Special Scientific Interest. The picnic place is civilized and the forest trail, which takes in an ancient landmark oak, won the Countryside Award in 1970, presented by Prince Philip. Salcey means willowy (Salicaceae), and the trail crosses some very wet ground where a considerable *salicetum* might well have flourished. Now only a few sallows remain, sycamore having taken hold in

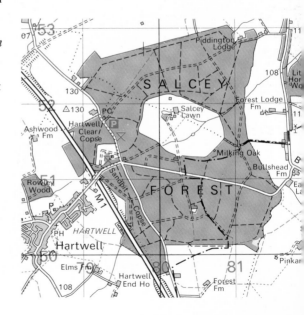

Near the car park provided by the Forestry Commission in Wakerley Great Wood

Eyebrook Reservoir on a cold March day

Coprinus disseminatus, fairy toadstools, open briefly into blue-grey 'daisies' before disappearing into the ground – Salcey Forest

the rides where, apparently an odd choice, the foresters have planted many English cherries and sweet chestnuts. There is a stand of giant fir, *Abies grandis* – this tree, happily, is being used increasingly in forestry. There is also *A. alba*, the common silver fir, now not very common. A 200-acre lawn in the middle of the forest is preserved, adding enormously to the potential habitat.

Perhaps one is always influenced by the weather: as the picture (page 35) shows this was a brilliant, slightly misty, early autumn morning which would have flattered the dullest surroundings; however, I think the forest walk would be very interesting and pretty even on a dull day. There are half a dozen ancient oaks left standing in various parts of the forest; one is even on the Ordnance Survey map – the Milking Oak.

The Church Path Oak, an ancient monument in Salcey Forest

41 42 43
35 **36** 37
20 21 22

CENTRAL ENGLAND
Cambridgeshire
Landranger sheets 141, 142, 153, 154

Hayley Wood *295 537, ♀, 150 acres, muddy, CNT*
Turn off the A14 (Ermine Street) at Longstowe, 9 miles north of Royston. At Longstowe are several fine elm trees – in flower in 1983 – though others are lost. The survival of these few is surprising considering that Wimpole Park, nearby, lost all its famous 2 miles of elms.

The way to the wood is signalled by a water tower and two white posts: you have to park at the roadside. A permit is needed from the Cambridge Naturalists' Trust to enter the wood, but much can be seen and learnt from the perimeter track, a public footpath. Coppicing is carefully controlled in the wood which is famous for its rich ground flora, particularly oxlips. Hayley is a classic ash-maple-hazel wood and has been much studied. As a walk, the footpath to Hayley, turning round the wood and then on to the disused railway to return, is a matter of taste. There was a thunderstorm when I explored: the breathless minutes before the storm, when birds began to seek the shelter of the trees, I would not have missed; the next half hour I could have done without.

Gamlingay Wood *239 539, ♀ ♣, about 160 acres, very muddy, pf*
Take the B1040 north out of Gamlingay: the wood is visible on your right, but the only way in is by a field track nearly opposite a gate of Waresley Park.

Parts of this old wood have been coniferized, but without obliterating the many stools of ash, oak and, here and there, maple. Patches of birch are on sand (deposited by wind over the Boulder Clay). Ash is now the commonest tree apart from the spruce and pine. There are a group or two of aspen, some hazel, some

Ash coppice, Gamlingay Wood

sallow. The floor is carpeted with dog's mercury, a very good green in early spring, and there is wood sorrel. A prominent bank in the more impenetrable northern part is covered with bluebells, as are several other drier patches, and the paths are full of primroses. Stout and weirdly shaped oaks remain on a low

bank surrounding the whole wood. Gamlingay has been the subject of various ecological studies, and it is well documented historically as a source of timber (large) as well as wood (small). Much clearing and felling is now being done. Its chief ornament to my eyes is its great collection of old ash stools, picturesque, mossy

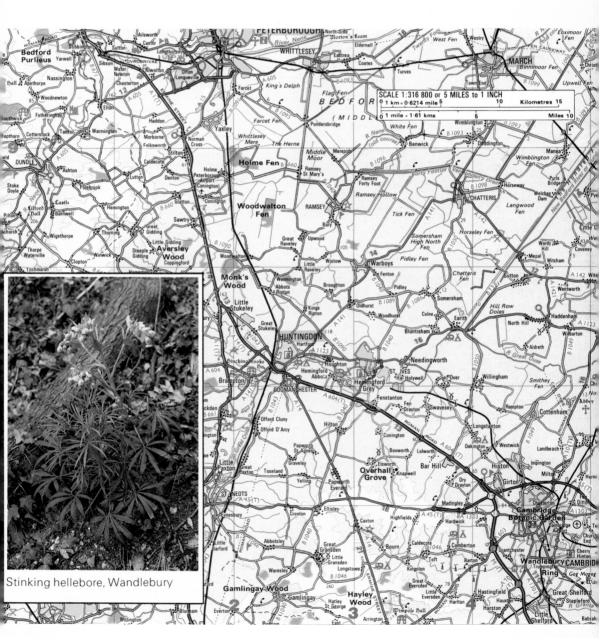

Stinking hellebore, Wandlebury

and sometimes fungus-covered. I had hoped to find more maple than in fact I did (in the south corner) and I did not come across the one reported wild service tree.

Turn right on entering the wood for the greater concentration of native trees and avoid the bridleway marked on the map. There are plenty of grassy rides.

Earth star fungus on ash stool, Gamlingay

Knapwell: Overhall Grove *337 633,* ♀, *43 acres, fp, NR*

The village of Knapwell has a historic 20 acres of woodland still with its ancient boundaries, first recorded in 1130, as discovered by Oliver Rackham. This wood is over a mile south of the present village street – near the A45(T). Mediaeval Knapwell was a large, busy place, its streets and gardens lined with pollard elms which have miraculously survived as 'old dodders' in the bumpy fields. The Manor, ruined long ago, lies immersed in secondary woodland, mostly of elm, which has spread from the Victorian-planted Grove, among ash, oak and maple. The earthworks are occupied by badgers.

Many but not all of the elms – it is the smooth-leaved elm – are dead, and the extra light in the wood will benefit the spring flowers for which the place is well known. A path wanders roughly parallel to the village street, muddy at the south end where it emerges at a style near a small pump house, at *334 624.*

ABOVE: elm coppice stool in Aversley Wood. LEFT: a Knapwell pollard of great age. RIGHT: smooth-leaved elm in a Cambridgeshire hedge.

ELM SURVIVORS

Many smooth-leaved elms have survived the elm disease epidemic in their native stronghold of the eastern Midlands. Only the wych elm, the other great survivor, sets fertile seed. The field elm, once common everywhere, does not coppice or pollard easily, as does the wych elm. Hybrids between the wych and other elms occurred in the warmer climate about 3000 BC and have reproduced by sucker shoots ever since, remaining roughly in the same place. Elms are thus of great historic interest. The old pollards of Knapwell mark the site of a large mediaeval village.

Bark of a rare pine, *Pinus gerardiana*, with visitor keeping a low profile, Cambridge Botanical Gardens

There are woodland corners, and many beautiful specimen trees and shrubs, in the **Cambridge Botanical Gardens**. Enter by Bateman Street, off Trumpington Road, less than a mile from King's College, to get the useful map leaflet. The gardens are closed on winter Sundays except to key-holders.

Wandlebury Ring *493 533*, ♀ *(♣), $\frac{3}{4}$m or $1\frac{1}{4}$m, very easy, Cambridge Preservation Trust*

Wandlebury is signposted on the A1307 (A604) 3 miles south of Cambridge. The Ring is the 1000-foot-diameter rampart and ditch of an Iron Age Fort, close to the Gog Magog Hills. The ramparts are planted with beech trees now large, and encircle the stable block of an eighteenth-century house now demolished. The estate of a hundred acres includes belts of woodland, of beech and oak, and there are several paths joining the woods.

Much planting has been done recently on the Ring, with a wide range of species to add to the existing pattern of box, yew, holly and beech. The ditch is full of elderberry: it was probably used to dump rubbish in former times and the chalky soil remains rich in nitrates. There is a great deal of ivy. Wild flowers were resplendent even in mid March: stinking hellebore and the naturalized winter aconite spreading beneath beeches; snowdrops

Beeches on Wandlebury Ring

in drifts; daffodils, not wild, in rather self-conscious clumps.

There is a wide south-sloping meadow for picnics, a pond with ducks tame enough to amuse anyone, and a shop (open Easter to October) with a booklet that probably tells you all about the archaeology of the Gog Magog Hills and a Roman road, now grassed over, that passes $\frac{1}{2}$ mile to the east. The stable clock is beautiful and the car park is nice.

There are not many woods in this wide, rolling chalk country.

Aversley Wood *165 818*, ♀, *152 acres, allow 2 hours, very muddy, WT*

The wood is now entirely owned by the Woodland Trust and access from Sawtry (by Manor House Farm) is feasible: the gate into the wood is in the middle of the south-east side.

Oak-ash woodland appears to have been the original vegetation on higher land in these parts, a somewhat featureless area of clay resembling rich cake and obviously very

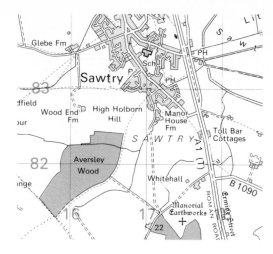

productive of food crops. But hills and clearings seem to have been synonymous in Saxon times, and Aversley ('Aefic's Lea') sounds like a clearing (near Sawtry, a 'salt-landing place' on the edge of the Fens). The presence of a large elm community in the middle of the south-west half also implies early

Artificial, but old, pond in Aversley Wood

clearing and habitation: the elms, now dead and in process of being cleared, were tall but grown up from old coppice stools, some of which have stout shoots and flowers in this year (1983). The tree is a wych elm hybrid. Elms dead at the north-east corner seem close in character (no leaves now available) but obviously did not coppice so freely: they probably invaded from the field hedge.

This is certainly a valuable acquisition for the Woodland Trust – but it is in rather a mess. Some good timber is being removed, and no doubt all the trees can look forward to good management after many years of living in a wilderness. There are good wild service trees, woodland hawthorn (*Crataegus laevigata*), and blackthorn as well as hazel, ash being slightly more common than its co-dominant oak, *Quercus robur*. Bluebells are everywhere, and there are many birds including at least one woodpecker. I disturbed a heron, a mallard and a moorhen on the pond in the centre. The rides are wide and more or less grassy. Jet planes were deafening.

Monks Wood, Woodwalton Fen and Holme Fen on the opposite side of the A1 are National Nature Reserves. **Monks Wood**, *201 797*, is guarded by the headquarters of the Institute of Terrestrial Ecology; you can ask them for a permit.

Holme Fen *215 884*, ♀ *, 640 acres, permit required for any thorough exploration, NNR*
Off the B660 which leaves the A1(T) eastwards, 2 miles north of Sawtry a typical fenland (dead straight) by-road leads into the wood by Middle Covert and Jackson's Covert. Here you can take a footpath into the wood to see the finest birch trees in lowland England. The trees have spread from areas planted in 1870 for game cover. They are certainly very beautiful.

Both Holme Fen and **Woodwalton Fen**, *234 849*, are subjects of elaborate scientific studies and one can understand the Nature Conservancy Council not encouraging casual picnicking, dog walking etc. Woodwalton is the only British home of a certain rare butterfly;

Holme Fen birches

also the history of the place is known since the Ice Age through fossil pollen preserved in its peat. Holme Fen was drained for agriculture, which later became impossible because of peat shrinkage (measurable at Holme Fen Post). Nature returned in the elegant form of *Betula pubescens*, with many grasses and rushes, birds and insects.

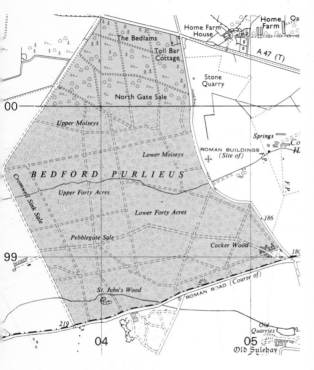

Bedford Purlieus *052 991,* ♀ ♣ , *many tracks, varying lengths, FC*
The Forestry Commission manages the intriguingly named Bedford Purlieus, 3 miles east of Wakerley. The map reference is approximately the best place to park, where a sandy lane leads to a piece of wasteland (and further if not too wet). The edges of the wood contain many concrete platforms and sinister-looking pits, the sort of thing the military are so good at making and so bad at removing. A purlieu is simply a piece of private land next to a forest – often only partly released from forest laws: a sort of forest suburb. The Bedford Purlieus holds the record for the number of vascular plant species it contains – approaching 400 – and has been described as a patchwork of woodland types. I visited it at the wrong season, but there was certainly a fine display of mosses. Coppices at the south contain sycamore and there is a great deal of birch, planted, much of it falling about in confusion: the occasional stands of conifers are much less neglected looking. A patch of lime coppice, *Tilia cordata*, is in the northern part beyond the conifers. Also coppiced generally are oak,

A muddy ride in the Purlieus

hazel, wych elm and ash, with scattered maple: some chestnut at the north and even a few horse-chestnuts.

A walk beginning at the east side and following the stream presents one with wych elm and sycamore, beech and oak, birch, and even a great hybrid lime, all in quick succession. This is the only part of the wood which has not suffered intensive management – or even, in one large area, temporary conversion to food-crop production. The rides provide some sort of plan; the wood is just large enough to make a compass useful if there is no sun, but on the whole the shade is light and plant hunters need not get lost. The wood was studied by Peterkin and Welch in 1975 and their publication *Bedford Purlieus: Its History, Ecology and Management* is available from the Institute of Terrestrial Ecology, 68 Hills Road, Cambridge, at a very reasonable cost.

North-West Suffolk

Landranger sheets 143, 144, 155

Thetford Forest. A desert of sand made into a forest of poles.

THETFORD FOREST

Thetford is the second largest forest in England, and almost all planted within the past sixty years – first with Scots pine, now with the higher-yielding Corsican pine. There are over 70 square miles of trees and nothing but trees, except for a total of 10 square miles of farmlands. This great natural machine projects into the air every day 555 tons of wet pinewood; more in summer, less in winter. A corresponding drier tonnage is delivered each day for sawing, for pitprops, woodwool, chipboard, pulp, fencing, telegraph poles and fuel, in that order of importance. The figures will nearly double by 1990. For every 200 tons of coal mined, the Forestry Commission tells us, 1 ton of pinewood props is used – an annual 23,000 cubic metres of peeled logs from Thetford Forest alone.

The plantation occupies about a fifth of the area of Breckland. This is the name of a very large sandy heath over flint and limestone, where the Scots pine was once a native, scattered tree – perhaps even a forest – destroyed by fires, natural or resulting from the clearings of early man. The prehistoric flint mines at Grimes Graves are in the middle of the present forest. The remaining Breckland heaths are converted to farmlands (where you can see the dust blowing in dry weather), or are occupied by the Army. Some original fragments are maintained (fences to keep the rabbits *in*) at Weeting Heath and Santon Warren.

It was the alien rabbit which in the seventeenth century finally removed much of the long over-grazed Breckland vegetation (heather, a few grasses, sand sedge and common reed). The few patches of pine which had held the whole thing together could not

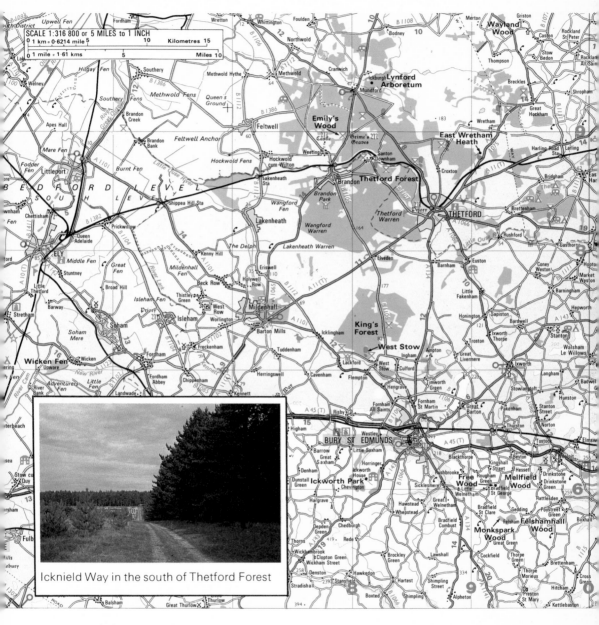

Icknield Way in the south of Thetford Forest

regenerate, their seedlings either too dry or eaten. As early as 1668 the village of Santon Downham was nearly buried in a catastrophic sandstorm. The region which had supported the earliest settlements of man in Britain became one of the least populated – the 'British Desert'. There may be a moral in that.

To **Santon Downham**, nowadays cool and leafy, you must go for Forestry Commission information: and it must be said that the Commission has done everything possible to welcome and entertain the visitor to the forest. The approach roads from the Thetford to Brandon road are magnificently shaded by broadleaved trees and there are very many, typically not-quite-secluded, parking areas on grass. At Santon are a small but good post office and stores, WCs with hot water, the old church of St Mary the Virgin, a pleasant open picnic site and an easy forest trail. Also a railway, a river, and, of course, the Forest Office, with leaflets, books and a small exhibition.

There are nine other picnic sites in the forest, most with marked walks and trails. If you despise laid-out walks you are free to explore all the Forestry Commission rides, but where the Commission only leases the land you are meant to stick to public rights of way. Be prepared for monotony, but that sort of monotony *may* be what you want! There is a long-distance walk of 23 miles marked with red posts from West Stow to High Ash through

varied country and including Grimes Graves and the Arboretum at Lynford (see below). No guide is published for this walk apart from the somewhat simplistic Guide Map for the forest.

Harling Drove was originally 14 miles of Stone Age track, later a drove road for cattle, and part is now a sandy public road through the woods from (west) 1 mile north of Brandon to (east) near Longmere. The Pilgrims' Walk, via St Helen's Well, roughly follows the Little Ouse.

An important nature reserve of original Breckland heath, meres and woodland is **East Wretham Heath**, 362 acres, *900 884*. The Drove Road between Longmere and Ringmore is open, but you need a permit to wander: apply to the Warden's office on the A1075 at 10 am or 2 pm (not on Tuesdays).

Weeting Heath, *755 881*, is a National Nature Reserve of 343 acres, mainly grassland.

On the Santon Downham trail

Emily's Wood *795 895*, ♀, *easy paths, FC*
This is a square mile of native hardwoods
acquired as part of a lot by the Forestry
Commission. The dominant pedunculate oak
flourishes here with every characteristic burr
and epicormic shoot, and a wealth of very
healthy-looking galls on bud and leaf.
Unusually large and small bunched leaves may
also be the result of galls, all of which are
caused by parasite wasps, midges and bugs for
the protection of their larvae – and often for
uninvited guests as well. The oak willingly
supports 284 different insects in Britain, the
alien spruce being much more at risk with only
37: the elm, with 80 native insects, succumbed
to just one beetle with its (imported) malignant
strain of fungus.

There is a group of large beeches at the west
side of the wood and the main path is marked
by lines of young beech. Prolific ash shoots in
less than their usually demanded light also
suggest the Forestry Commission's hand
improving on nature; but we should not
complain. Healthy wych elms were still found
in 1982, and you can see some fascinating fungi
of dead ash and oak.

The wood is indicated by a picnic site
2 miles out of Brandon on the A1065 to
Swaffham. The roadside is lined with Norway
maples – and much evidence of temporary
settlement by *Homo sapiens*. But don't let this
put you off; Emily's Wood is lovely, and you
may have it all to yourself on a fine afternoon in
spring or autumn.

Lynford Arboretum *822 942*, ♀ ♣, *easy,*
FC
Lynford Hall is signposted a few hundred
yards from the Mundford roundabout on the
A1065 to Swaffham. Drive on past the hall and
the 'Executive Mobile Homes'. Just beyond
these is the compact arboretum, which we
have mapped as an example of a good small
conifer collection. There are some hardwoods,
none particularly rare, the main value of
Lynford being the comparatively young
specimen conifers – as against the decayed and
overgrown atmosphere of many Victorian
plantations. (Not that the 'Big Tree',
Sequoiadendron, which you can see here, is

Tree-eating fungi in Emily's Wood and, TOP, an
oak tree

anything but juvenile anywhere in Britain:
introduced in 1853, it will not reach adulthood
before 2100, and may live until AD 4000.)

Labelling of the specimen trees has yet to be
properly done by the Forestry Commission,
which has kindly provided a plan for our use:
some trees are missing, presumed frostbitten,
and there are a few which I cannot identify,

48

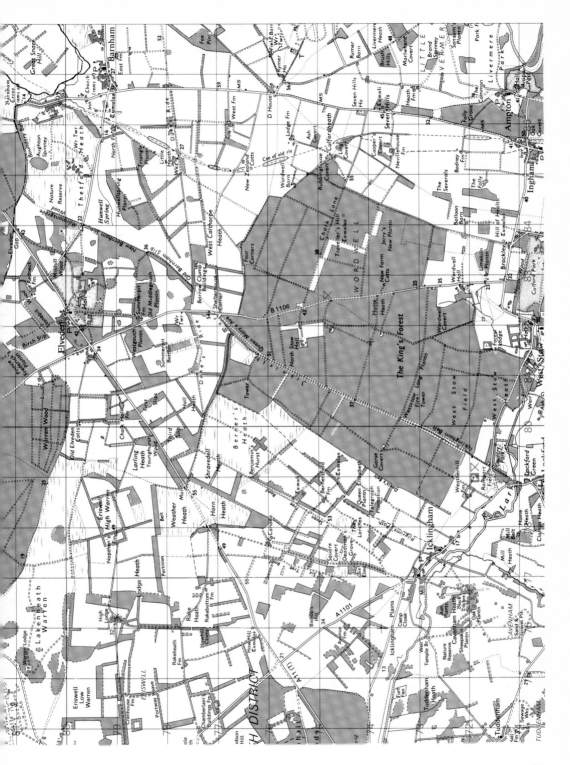

49

Spruces and cypresses in Lynford Arborteum

notably a charming pendulous 'white' spruce at the west side. A secondary attraction of Lynford is that you do not have to walk more than about 200 paces to find a particular group. Many large and shapely Scots pines, the original and oldest trees planted here, are not indicated on the plan. There are picnic benches in the open land towards the lake. Very easy walking, but much long wet grass.

The forest continues north beyond Ickburgh (High Ash), where there are camping sites, and there is a large patch south-west of Swaffham; picnic site on the A1122 with attached walks. Outlying plantations to the east have picnic sites, with walks, on the A1075 (Hockham Forest) and off the A1066 (Bridgham Lane).

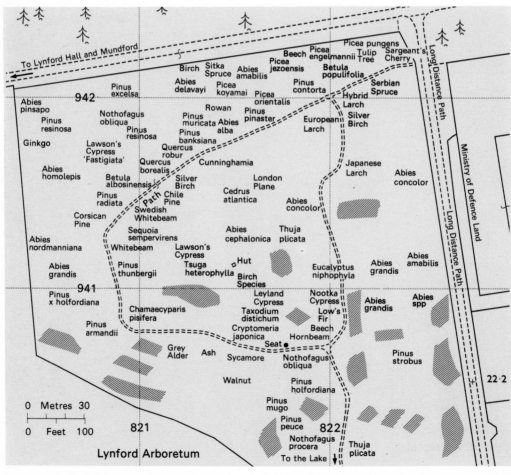

The names refer to single trees or small groups. Old pines (Scots pine) etc are indicated by patches of shade. Not all the specimens named may have survived and there may be specimens not named but the relation of one group to another is roughly as indicated.

West Stow forest trail

West Stow *815 705*, ♠ (♀), *long and short walks, FC* and **Icknield Way**

The Forest Office for the southern part of Thetford Forest is at the north of this pretty village, beyond the secluded detached residences of Bury St Edmunds' commuters. The long-distance walk begins here and penetrates The **King's Forest**, as does Icknield Way from Lackford Bridge. Here a wide ride, the Way is leafy at first, then in solid Corsican pine, but the ride is bordered by nurse trees of birch and beech and some old sweet chestnut. Clumps of broom and Coca Cola cans break the monotony, frequent jet planes break the silence .. but the forest is mighty.

There is easy parking at Rampart Field, *788 715*, on the A1101 (Suffolk County Council) for the Icknield Way, or a little further along the West Stow road, *802 713*, where a very interesting Anglo-Saxon village is being reconstructed (open 11 am at weekends, 2 pm weekdays) near hills formed by municipal waste (but you'd never guess). The river bank here provides a recommendable walk bordered by grown-up alder coppice, old ashes, attractive white willows, the small woods still called Alder Carr, Ash Carr – this being the traditional name for wetland scrub. Good place to tip rubbish, I suppose they thought: but all has been made pure again, and clumps of suitable trees are planted and tended.

Returning to West Stow itself there is a shortish (two hours?) trail with yellow posts which proceeds prettily through plots of various ages of pine after a dramatic start in the deep twilight of a stand of Douglas fir.

AROUND BURY ST EDMUNDS

Ickworth Park *812 619*, near Bury, has several woods and acres of National Trust parkland, open always, not perhaps competing in interest with the house, which has a colossal oval rotunda and curving wings. Lancelot Brown did some work in the grounds.

Mellfield Wood *925 605*, has a footpath right of way through the middle running east to west, which continues through **Free Wood** to Bradfield St George. However, new houses

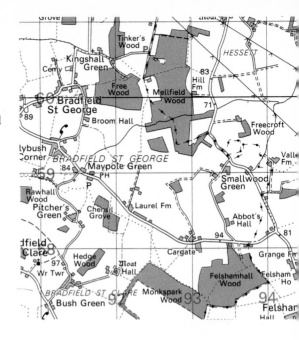

at Bradfield St George have made the footpath awkward to locate. I parked on the Beyton to Felsham road. The footpath notice had been removed with the hedge, I was told, but the entrance to the wood can be seen at a slight angle in its outline. The farmer was removing more hedge (leaving a finely shaped oak by the ditch) and I am not sure that any crossing will be available – be prepared to jump. Alternative routes will be clear from the map, and you can plan a round walk. The north end of Mellfield Wood is coppice of long standing, hazel and elm, and some cutting is being done. An old stone road, half buried, crosses here, and the ground flora could be interesting in the next few years. All sorts of management seem to have been tried in the wood – some conifers – and there is a fine stand of hybrid poplars near Free Wood Farm, which itself has the air of belonging to another century, not because of any architectural feature but just by its ambience. Please do not try to invade by car.

Bradfield Woods *935 581*, ♀, *160 acres, NNR*

Felshamhall Wood, which is on the road from Bradfield St George to Gedding, is of

great interest. With part of the adjoining
Monkspark Wood it is scheduled in the
highest category of National Nature Reserves.
Oliver Rackham, in his *Ancient Woodland*,
1980, describes these woods as a microcosm of
the ancient woods of England. Coppicing here
is recorded as 'before 1252' and there is an
unbroken record of management up to the
present. Monkspark Wood was not coppiced:
it was a deer park.

Monkspark Wood was known more recently
for its white admirals and bush crickets, and in
1929 was proposed as a National Nature
Reserve, but the plan was shelved. In 1966
two-thirds of the south-western part of the
wood were grubbed up for conversion to
agriculture before local people managed to stop
the process and obtain a tree-preservation
order. In 1970, through the generosity of
many, the whole of Felshamhall Wood and the
remains of Monkspark Wood were acquired as
a potential National Nature Reserve.

The reserve is a working wood yielding most
woodland products and retaining its 'social
links'. Particular sizes of underwood are used
by a factory that makes rakes, scythe-sticks and
articles of turnery. The woods yield poles and
stakes and thatching wood of various kinds,
and supply the neighbourhood with fuel. Even
the twigs are not wasted, for the ashes of
bonfires are collected and sold to potters for
use in glazes.

There are 370 flowering plants and ferns
including 42 native trees and shrubs, this being
two-thirds of all British native trees and shrubs.
The woods are almost entirely ancient – some
patches of recent origin on old meadows and
launds. The underwood varies from new-cut to
30 years' growth, and standard trees, mainly
oak, ash, birch and alder, are usually less than
70 years old, thinly and evenly scattered.
Felshamhall Wood has an ancient wood-bank
boundary, with pollard trees.

Plant communities are complex and they
interpenetrate over very varied soils: acidity
varies from pH 3.1 to 7.4 (from highly acid to
calcareous), almost the maximum possible in
Britain. A calcareous patch is on the Gedding
side behind the cottage, and the most acid
areas are in the centre and beyond the Fish

(shaped) Pond in Monkspark Wood near its
new boundary at the south-west.

Please do not take a dog unless it is
impeccably trained in woodland behaviour.

The Suffolk countryside is lovely, intimate and
open by turns. On a really nasty day you could
do worse than walk on the Drinkstone to
Gedding road, which is quiet, and not without
pubs, and bordered almost the whole way by
thick shelter-belt woodland. Or you could park
near Timworth, 3 miles to the north of Bury St
Edmunds, and follow the farm roads which
here border fields and woods in open, gently
undulating countryside.

Wicken Fen *562 705,* ♀ ⚘*, 700 acres, usually wet in places, NT*

The National Trust's oldest property, dating
from 1899, this is a remnant of the Great Fen
of East Anglia, now drained. Wicken remains
as an oasis of wetland where once all was wet,
except for a few 'islands' – so called
traditionally. Water is pumped up from the
surrounding land into the fen: the Wicken
windmill, built to drain the land, now works to
keep it wet, aided at times by a diesel pump.

A sedge and reed fen is not any sort of
woodland, nor is it a 'natural' form of
vegetation, for without its regular autumn cut
the sedge and reed would be colonized by fen
carr of alder buckthorn, guelder rose, sallows,
hawthorn, privet, and then by ash, oak and
elm. (Alder appears not to regenerate here.)
Wicken offers not exactly a woodland, rather a
potential woodland which is never going to be
allowed to develop. There are, however,
patches and borders of woodland trees. Also,
one small triangle, dedicated to Sir Harry
Godwin, the great palaeobotanist, has been left
alone for study, and a larger section, Wicken
Poors' Fen, is not managed by the Trust.

The fen is an example of undrained fenland
– calcareous peat over clay – virtually
unparalleled in all of Europe. With all its
individual plant life and history, the fen is the
habitat of, it is claimed, 300 flowering plants,
5000 insect species including 700 moths and
butterflies (the British subspecies of
swallowtail butterfly has been reintroduced

In Wicken Fen

here), 200 spiders, six known nowhere else, and many birds including the bittern, shoveler, smew and goosander. In the woodland are species of woodpecker, and in the fen redpoll, reed-warbler and sedge-warbler and many other small birds.

Some 'droves' (wide pathways) are very ancient, maybe even Roman. The whole Fenland was farmed by the Romans until the final rise in sea-level, about the fourth century, made habitation difficult.

Birches, grey poplars, alders and, probably, elms are not native vegetation but date from planting at the turn of the century by the then private owners. Beyond the Brickpits (now open water, with water milfoil, bladderwort and both white and yellow water-lilies) there is a row of willows which grew up from fencing stakes. Guelder rose, a native shrub, grows by the water here. Its bark was formerly used to relieve the cramps suffered by workers in the wetlands.

The guide available at the Warden's house gives a full 2-mile itinerary.

Wayland Wood *925 995,* ♀ *, permit required, CNT*
This is reputedly the 'Babes in the Wood' woodland, but it belongs to the Norwich Naturalists' Trust. (Apply to 72 The Close, Norwich, for a permit.) It is a secretive place, not to be disturbed by noisy parties, dogs, or, particularly, babes. In a coppice clearing, ash trunks gleam around large bushes of lesser burdock almost of tree proportions. It is an ash/oak wood mainly, with hazel, and, if you can find it, bird cherry.

This is a very old wood, its name coming from the Viking *Wane(s)lund. Lundr* was a grove, suggesting that this wood was distinct as far back as the late eighth century. A clearing in forest land would have been *thwaite*, a name common in Yorkshire, Derbyshire and the Lakes.

SCALE 1:316 800 or 5 MILES to 1 INCH

Blo Norton Wood *030 788*, ♀, *CNT*

An oakwood with sweet chestnut, birch and some conifers, and a lot of stinkhorns in autumn, it provides 10 minutes' easy walking on the bridleway at the western end; elsewhere adopt a crouching pose. There is woodland also at Redgrave nearby and at Bruisyard (coniferized) and Heveningham. The last is the interesting old park, with ancient thorns and others, of a great house.

Dunwich Forest, *462 713*, is a large, easy-

going pine plantation, with Walberswick Marshes and nature reserve to the east and north. This is a holiday coast: take things as you find them. A Forestry Commission picnic place is ¾ mile from Dunwich village. There are many sandy footpaths and nature trails: Dunwich Common on the Sandlings is heathland, but there is woodland attached to the RSPB reserves of Minsmere and North Warren – north of Aldeburgh.

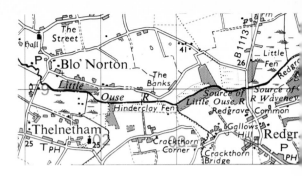

Rendlesham Forest ♠, *several easy walks, FC*

This is a vast forest, inland from Aldeburgh and Orford. Picnic places, particularly at Sandgalls, *380 560* (on the Iken road from Tunstall), are by no means all 'honeypots' to keep the swarms of ignorant townspeople out of trouble. The large car park at Butley Corner, *354 502* (in Rendlesham Forest on the Orford road from Woodbridge and Melton),

Holly stool of landscape proportions in Butley Thicks

offers, wisely without any mention, an anchorage for those who would embark on the best and the worst woodland walk in Britain, in Butley Thicks. Best because the oak and holly wood have remained strangely undisturbed for centuries; worst because walking in anything like an erect posture is impossible. It is private, but well known to naturalists. A little-used bridleway goes by the west side of the Thicks and into the park.

Staverton Park and **Butley Thicks** formed a deer forest in the thirteenth century and they have reputedly not been touched since. Many deer parks were grazed to semi-deserts, so something must have gone wrong – or right. Some people believe these woods to be a fragment of original English forest. This cannot be so, since most of the trees in the Thicks have been coppiced at some time, and any sort of clearing alters the woodland ecology. The enormous size of some holly stools – 4 or 5 feet across – certainly suggests ages of 300 years or more, and this is, of course, almost unknown for a holly. All the oaks are extremely picturesque and there are ancient

coppiced rowans and ashes as well.

Tunstall Common, *378 548*, is a fine open place, remarkably free of rubbish and notices about rubbish. The colours are of heather, sand, bracken-gold or green, and gorse; and beyond, the fine orange-pink and blue of Scots pines, not too geometrically laid out, but with trunks as straight as rulers. There is another open heath at Blaxhall, to the north. You can walk anywhere.

As one learns to expect in the 'quiet' places of eastern England, there are frequent roars and whistles from the latest and most lethal jet planes.

Tunstall Common, Scots pine

Stafford and Shrewsbury

Landranger sheets 126, 127

Attingham Park, Shrewsbury *542 093, ♀, 3826 acres, 1m walk, NT*

The map reference is for the main gate on the A5(T) near the bridge at Atcham. The house is open in summer months, but the park has the virtue of being always open. It was designed by Repton, but this need not inhibit one's appreciation of its wide spaces and well-marked groups of trees – Humphrey Repton could hardly have looked ahead for 200 years, though I believe his intentions have been respected.

The classical façade of pale grey stone is beautifully balanced by the group of oaks and chestnuts at its side. The effect transcends mere classicism and looks other-worldly and poetical on a sunny, misty morning; and, I dare say, in most other lights. Cedars behind the building are silhouetted against the unexpected hump of The Wrekin to the east – and one notices that young cedars are well grown, ready to replace the old. Dramatic shadows cloak the rear entrance under its cupola – there is a miniature forest of butcher's

broom under the beeches – and the driveway seems to enter an entirely different world from ours. It is a very convincing sort of stage set, and makes one shiver for an instant in the breath of a distant era. What more can one ask of a National Trust property?

There is a walk of 1 mile signposted behind the stable block, which leads into the trees.

The Wrekin *634 093, ♀ ↟, 1½ hours easy walking but steep, MoD*

Only the most conspicuous of the series of outcrops of ancient limestone which distinguishes this part of the country, The Wrekin, 1300 feet high, accommodates a sessile oak coppice, a beechwood, and a rifle range on its north-west side, above a birchwood containing more than its fair share of rubbish. The south side is largely covered by larchwood. The lesser Lawrence's Hill, to the north-east, has large quarry workings. Below is the M54, Hadley to the north and Dawley to the east. 'The birthplace of industry', we are told on entering Telford.

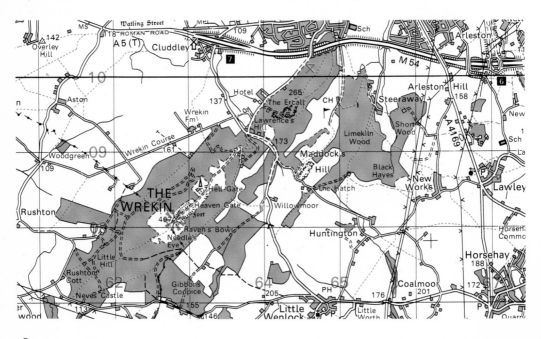

Turning off this M54 at junction 7 towards The Wrekin, it is best then to turn right – signposted Uppington – where appears at once a rough parking place under the birches. Climbing straight up through the coppice brings you to an easy, broad path, lined with beech, leading to the summit and a fine view.

Cannock Chase (west) *982 175 (Chase Road Corner car park),* ♀ ♣ , *2700 acres CP, 6000 acres FC*
Entering the area from Cannock you may be reassured by a series of very clear signs to a 'Visitor Centre'. Take no notice, they simply lead you to Rugeley through miles of

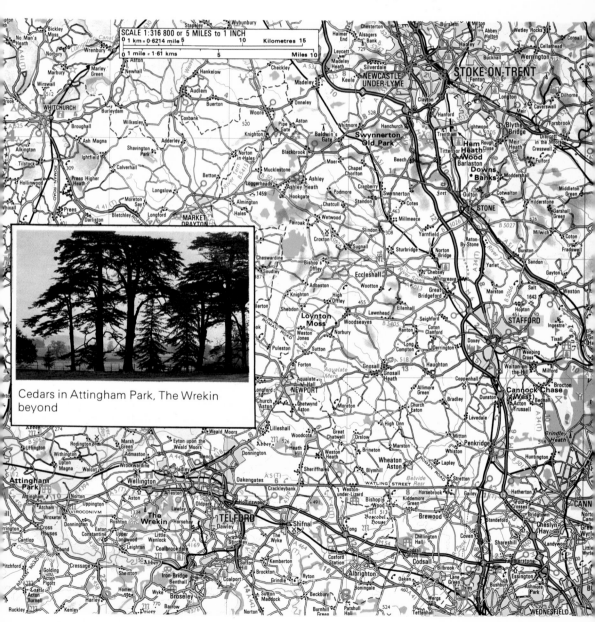

Cedars in Attingham Park, The Wrekin beyond

monotonous forestry. You will not then be surprised to be informed, in Forestry Commission pokerwork, that the conifers yield 33 tons a day.

To the north of Pye Green (the southern limit of the Chase, marked by a Post Office tower) are car parks at Brindley Bottom, *993 153*, Flints Field, *995 156*, and Whitehouse, *995 162*. These are all in the Corsican pine belt, but there are open spaces: there is nothing much to choose between one car park and another.

Going north from Pye Green but forking left, past the Post Office tower, takes you towards the Country Park area of much more open birch heath broken by stands of pine.

On The Wrekin. Early-morning mist.

Quite without identification except for a
15 mph limit, the Chase Road turns off right at
966 184, leading to several car parks and a
viewpoint before descending to Brocton at the
north of the Chase. A through footpath, the
Staffordshire Way, runs south to north parallel
to, and east of, the Chase Road. The path
follows the Sherbrook Valley and leads on to

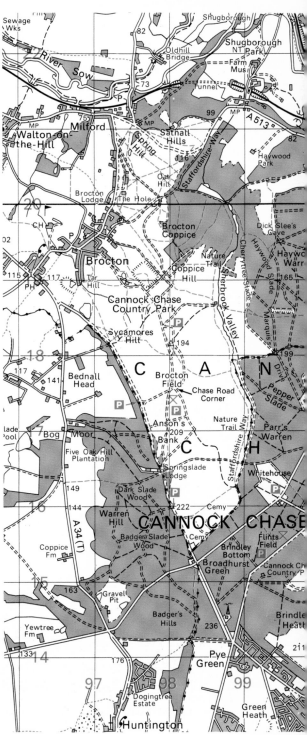

Shugborough Park (National Trust, 900 acres with neo-Georgian monuments), or, if you turn off left or north-west, spills out into the uneven acres of Milford Common – an attractive destination.

A large-scale walkers' map published by the Staffordshire County Council was not available to us, and my explanations are necessarily limited. On balance it seems that the Chase Road Corner car park, map reference given above, will take you to the centre of interest. Or turn to Section 40 for a striking eastern viewpoint also arranged by Staffordshire County Council.

Scattered woods, totalling a considerable acreage, between Market Drayton and Stoke-on-Trent are all in Forestry Commission hands. There is a picnic place at Harley Thorns, in **Swynnerton Old Park**, *838 396*. **Downs Banks,** near Barlaston, is a moorland National Trust site of 166 acres: *902 370*. **Hem Heath Wood**, Trentham, *885 410*, is a woodland nature reserve of 20 acres leased

from the National Coal Board, rich in tree and shrub species.

Many woods also are in the hands of the Staffordshire NCT.

Loynton Moss *791 246,* ♀ *, 33 acres, NR*
The Shropshire Union Canal north of picturesque Norbury Junction runs in a deep cutting full of quite mature trees, and here passes under what used to be an aqueduct, now a footbridge: this you cross. Calcareous clay banks were thrown up in digging the canal, while the moss shows a 'marked transition from fen to acid bog', to quote the *Nature Reserves Handbook*. It was only recently under water – surely an odd place for a canal cutting? When I visited the site it was nearly dark and I can only record that it is unusually beautiful, fairly wet, and that some of the trees are coppiced alders. I was able to identify the 'cones' by touch. On the whole I recommend a daylight visit. Your walk might continue along the canal towpath in either direction (pubs are equidistant, $1\frac{1}{2}$ miles).

Cannock Chase. Birches near Chase Road.

45	46	47
39	**40**	41
33	34	35

CENTRAL ENGLAND
Trent and Churnet
Landranger sheets 128, 129

Calke and Staunton Harold Reservoir
379 220, ♀ ♣, *parking place*

The reservoir is a place for views, and there is a viewpoint car park, *376 227*, beyond the village of Calke, where you can succumb to the effects, whatever they are, of gazing at a sheet of water. A very nice car park at the map reference is on a wooded hillside shaded by vivid yellow hybrid poplars. The ridge above leads by a semi-official footpath to Staunton Harold Hall, National Trust, with a nice mixture of trees and grass above the shapely valley: invigorating on a windy day. To the east, Breedon on the Hill continues the theme of Charnwood Forest, here charmingly formalized by a church set on a scrub-patterned hill, great cooling towers beyond.

Parks. The castle is just a big house, with an ancient corner. The gardens and grounds are in the grand manner with old, well-kept topiary, very geometrical. Look west of the chapel for a group of Irish yews, birches, pencil cedars and other larger conifers: all beautifully organized and good of their kind. There is a short walk laid out in the trees flanking the Grand Avenue – which looks south, the lawn delicately ramped to hide the road. The park is always open and can be entered on foot at Elvaston, Borrowash or the Golden Gates on the A6(T).

By Staunton Harold Reservoir

Elvaston Castle *412 332,* ♀ ♣, *200 acres, CP*

The parking place is just south-east of the castle, 200 yards from the minor road which passes it. Elvaston was one of the first Country

Cannock Chase (east) *039 153*
(viewpoint, car park and picnic place), ♀ ♣ ,
CC, FC

The large area of Cannock Chase, one of the
largest accessible tracts of wooded country in
England, is on this side Foresty Commission
managed, but the viewpoint given is cared for
by Staffordshire County Council. It is an old
gravel-pit hill looking over forestry and
industry and in any but the dullest light is most
appealing. Take the Hazelslade road from the
A51 in Brereton, and turn sharp right as soon
as you reach the trees.

The Forestry Commission's Forest Centre,

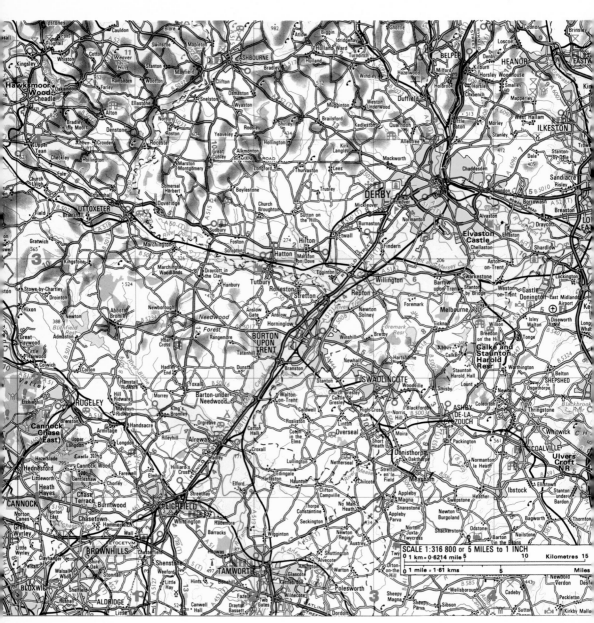

From the viewpoint at *039 153*, Cannock Chase (east)

A stand of beech in Cannock Chase Forest

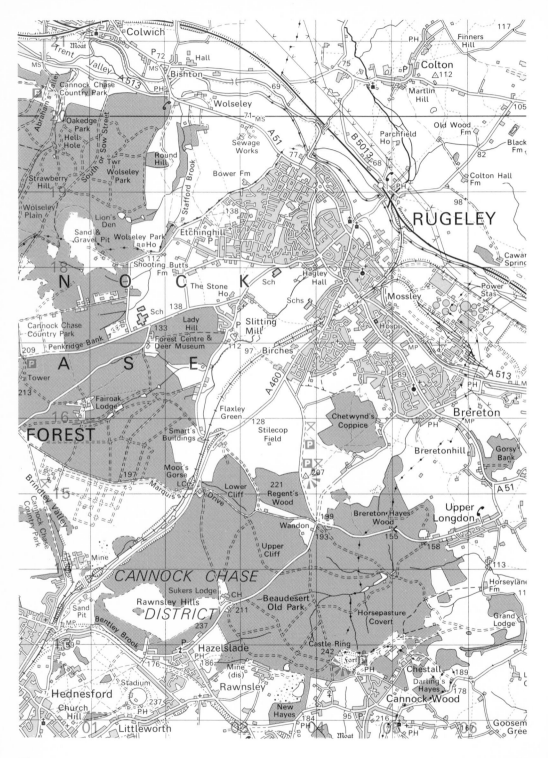

018 171, is educational in purpose and displays statistics amongst the pines; '$\frac{1}{2}$ million trees ... annual growth 22,000 tons. Daily harvest 33 tons'. There are trails. For older deciduous woodland go south of our viewpoint above. All the woods are open, but to plan your walk you need a map.

A Forestry Commission car park called Penkridge (why? The town is 5 miles to the west) offers a 3-mile walk with red markers, and as this is close to yet another of those Army firing ranges, you had better follow the markers.

Churnet Valley

In the north-west of the section the River Dove is the boundary of Staffordshire. The River Churnet joins the Dove below Alton Towers, and above this landmark is heavily wooded, especially near Oakamoor, the Forestry Commission being mostly in charge. A National Trust woodland, **Hawksmoor Wood**, *033 440*, with a separate patch to the north-west by Wood House Farm, occupies the north-east-facing valley side, opposite a conspicuous, loudly humming factory. The wood is dull, but of course is a valuable bird sanctuary, if birds don't mind humming noises. Old trees, oaks, beeches, rowans, are only at the margins. By the B5417, at the south-east corner and the obvious entry point, a triangle of old quarry land, outside the property, is neglected and rubbishy. Sandstone and gravel strata are well exposed. It could form an excellent stopping place, but besides bulldozer work would need a footbridge over the road to the wood. The photograph, taken from the north-west boundary of the wood, looks up the Churnet Valley: it flatters the wood by excluding the factory, but shows the character of the valley.

This is a large wood, 307 acres, at present of more importance as a natural refuge than as a place to walk.

The RSPB has a large reserve in the Coombes Valley, upstream: *009 534* – old estate woodland with thick rhododendron in places, as well as pasture and heathland. The reserve is not open on Mondays, Wednesdays and Fridays (and no weekdays in autumn), and is closed in January, February and March. There is an entrance fee and you should report to the Information Centre.

The Churnet Valley and the edge of Hawksmoor Wood

Charnwood Forest: scrubland and granite wall in Ulverscroft nature reserve

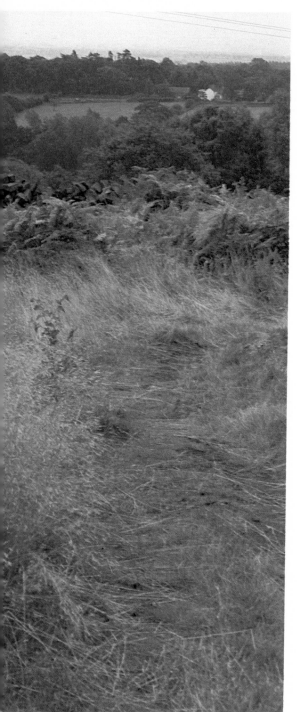

Woodland walk in Ulverscroft nature reserve

Ulverscroft, Copt Oak *488 125,♀, 120 acres, 1½ hour walk, NR*

Described as the richest valley in Charnwood
Forest, with woodland the breeding site of the
wood warbler, this is a varied, mostly
scrubland nature reserve which well deserves
the name. The entrance is in the wood about a
mile down Whitcroft's Lane, off the B591
¼ mile south of Copt Oak. Apart from the
scrub, which is heavy with bracken but
contains quite mature birch and rowan
(including the oldest rowan I have seen), there
are small beech plantations enclosed by walls
of the angular, hard-looking pre-Cambrian
stone: walls and beeches alike are mostly an
acrid green. Pedunculate oaks, planted in the
woods, have spread to the scrub. There are
patches of heather, gorse and bramble
frequented by many flies, wasps and
butterflies. A pond is almost unbelievably rich
in insect life and smells awful. Waymarks,
arrows on posts, give some guidance for a walk
of about one and a half hours.

CENTRAL ENGLAND
Charnwood, Belvoir and
Ermine Street   Landranger sheets 129, 130

CHARNWOOD FOREST

Leicestershire has been short of woodlands since before Domesday and there has been some doubt as to how the people obtained any wood at all: there must have been a fairly extensive Leicester forest. Perhaps part of Rutland Forest also supplied the very necessary wood. The Leicester Forest, anyway, was sold by Charles I for £7000. North-west towards Ashby-de-la-Zouch, a hilly area with outcrops, or islands, of ancient sandstone, and some of the most ancient and hardest rocks and slates, became known as Charnwood Forest. It was the waste of manors of Whitwick, Groby, Shepshed and Barrow, and by the end of the eighteenth century it had become little more than heath and bracken; extensively quarried,

it was a forest of stones, not trees. It was enclosed under an Act of Parliament in 1808 by various owners, who planted trees here and there.

Swithland Wood *537 117*, ♀, *with Bradgate Park 1238 acres, many paths, CP* Swithland Wood is I believe ancient. The oaks are sessile and some old stubs, the remains of coppice trees, clearly predate the Inclosure period. The land has been much disturbed by quarrying and birch has spread; but, while many of the oaks may have been planted, the whole has grown up into a very fine woodland. The many paths lead in all directions, not clarified by yellow-painted posts.

A deep quarry full of water is fenced off with old-style palings. Swithland's slate is

Swithland Wood, English oaks

apparently well known. Probably it was the quarrying interest which ensured the survival of the coppice. The wood was preserved for the nation in 1931 by the Leicester Rotarians, who perhaps remembered boyhood expeditions and by then owned nice houses in the district: an enlightened gesture all the same.

Bradgate Park, *523 116,* just south of the wood, is easy to find in the middle of Newton Linford. The house is ruined. There are picturesque oaks in the park, and a herd of deer. The Visitors' Centre, Marion Cottage, is open on some summer afternoons.

The **Outwoods,** *515 159,* are oak and

Clipsham yew

conifer woodlands in a nature reserve of the ridge above the Soar Valley.

The nature reserve of Ulverscroft, 120 acres, is just off the map to the west, at *488 125*. See Section 40. The Leicester and Rutland Trust for Nature Conservation controls at least four important woodlands, including the large (300 acres) Pickworth Great Wood, but you need permits to visit these.

LEICESTERSHIRE/LINCOLNSHIRE

Some Forestry Commission sites just off the A1(T) to the east offer riches unexpected on this uneventful stretch of road.

Morkery Wood *955 193, (♀)✦, 600 acres, 1 short walk and forest rides, FC*
100 miles from London is this great army of conifers, spruce and pine, with a fringe of oak and beech and the inevitable ash, the hedgerow tree of the district. Turn off the A1 for Castle Bytham. The 'farm' marked on the map to the south is in fact an HM prison, and the road through the forest is thus a dead-end and an extension of the parking area. It is enlivened by a mysterious stone carved with a horse and a lot of orchid and yellow vetch. The picnic place offers both shade and (an old quarry) a

place in the sun. There is a short track which, the Forestry Commission claims, follows old deer trails.

Clipsham Yew Avenue *980 170, a short walk, FC*
A yew avenue is not exactly a woodland walk but this remarkable, large-scale topiary is worth seeing on any account. The yews are 200 years old. The car park, quiet and secluded, has a more rapidly run-up backdrop of Lawson cypress. This is a lovely place. The bit of Kesteven Forest beyond the yew avenue is a young assemblage of smart spruces and vigorous pines, and the rides or firebreaks are dreamy corridors of grasses, marsh orchids and small native trees framing the large skies. There are oaks, ashes, maples and even wild service trees along an informal pathway which leaves the parking place, follows the northern margin and turns left and left again along the rides, returning to the yew avenue about midway down its length. At the western or home end of the avenue, full of 6-foot nettles, is a tall, dying elmwood: beautiful without being attractive. These elms have grown up from old coppice.

A mile south-east is **Holywell Wood**, private, and the quietest place in England –

Swithland slate tip

Thuja plicata in an English oak-ash wood, Ropsley Rise

even the rabbits go on eating as you approach them. Only tentatively coniferized, this is a wood of oak, ash, hazel, maple, birch, aspen, elder, hawthorn, guelder rose, dog rose and wayfaring tree, roughly in that order. There is a right-of-way through from the farm at *986 156* continuing through the adjoining **Pickworth Great Wood** to the village of Pickworth. The right-of-way gives no right to deviate from it; please do not go this way unless you intend to be perfectly quiet and please do not take a dog.

Twyford Wood *946 238, (♀)♠*,
700 acres, ½m walk plus miles of concrete runway, FC

Preserving the blunt triangle of the wartime airfield on which it was planted, the wood is largely of youngish, regimented conifers as you might expect, but the walk meanders first through a rich variety of native trees as well as plunging into small darknesses of silver fir and hemlock. Ragged robin, comfrey and guelder rose grow by the spruces. Fallow deer browse in the remains of the RAF's bomb store. On the runways the spruces stretch away in enormous vistas: a good place to jog.

Ropsley Rise Wood *972 347,* ♀ ♠,
150 acres, ½m trail, FC

Badgers, foxes and long-eared owls may be seen, says the Forestry Commission. The picnic place is reached by a minor road from the A52 soon after it leaves Ermine Street at Cold Harbour: you can see the wood from the A52. It is a pleasant, open wood flanked by a ditch full of sallows and a variety of rushes, with horsetail and some orchids of the *Dactyloryhiza* genus, common marsh orchid, here pale mauve. The walk progresses through scented red cedars, *Thuja plicata*, to attractive young firs, *Abies grandis*, all planted amongst ash and oak and with plenty of native undergrowth. The larger part of the wood is of spruce – here rights are reserved. Until the cedars and firs grow up the trail part is a fine nature reserve.

Rutland Water, west of the A1 near Oakham, the largest man-made lake in England (about

TOP: guelder rose, a native shrub of wetland, Clipsham. CENTRE: ragged robin, Twyford Wood. ABOVE: white comfrey in Twyford Wood.

$4\frac{1}{2}$ square miles), ought to be mentioned. It has fine woodland belonging to Burley Park at the north side; to enter this wood you have to apply for a permit. In the circumstances this is reasonable (the circumstances are parking areas for about 2000 cars). There is a scrap or two of wood near the lake, with sycamore much in evidence. A fine cherry has a notice nailed to it about hiring something or other. There is a monumentally well-designed, air-conditioned WC. An arboretum keeps a very low profile as it is only six years old and about 2 acres in extent. It contains named specimens of the native trees used in their thousands for planting around the reservoir, in 1975. A nature reserve 9 miles long goes all round the water, but there is no woodland walk as such yet: water birds are the interest. Planting birches, alders and rowans is in good taste I suppose, but the whole affair is so artificial that I feel the Water Authority has lost an opportunity of creating a grand coniferous landscape, perhaps of species not normally used in forestry, which would have added to the transformation of the scene – creating a bit of romantic Switzerland. The thousands of indigenous trees will be fine when they mature, but they are by way of an apology for all that has been lost under water. At least we could have both – it is not too late to think in terms of a block or two of, say, Greek firs, Atlas cedars or Serbian spruces.

NEAR GRANTHAM

Belvoir: Terrace Hills Woods *797 321,* ♀ *(♣), 1½m of the Jubilee Way, easy and dry* The map reference takes you to a minor road where the Jubilee Way walk crosses and there is a triangle of grass for parking. You can also park at the castle entrance on 'hard standing', free, or along the Knipton road where several parking places have been sculpted out of the bank under large beeches and hornbeams. Knipton, and in fact the whole surrounding country in a 2-mile radius, is outstanding for fine wayside trees, shelter-belts of larch, even clumps of cedars, while *Araucaria* (monkey puzzle) and *Sequoiadendron* (Wellingtonia) stand in the corn fields. Monkey puzzles turn

up again in the oakwood of the Terrace Hills along the walk, with really fine sycamores and horse-chestnuts, and rhododendron as a quite welcome understorey in place of the fearsome nettles which flourish here. You can start the walk from the Knipton road end, along a green road – all is clearly signposted.

The castle has a nature trail, but you have to pay to get in, and since the place always has junketing of one sort or another going on (jousting for instance), nature seems a secondary consideration.

North of Grantham another great park, **Belton**, *929 395,* on the A607, also has nature trails (lakeside) among any number of other activities: again there is a fairly steep charge to drive in. Typically the trees are large and well formed.

Belvoir Castle and the Terrace Hills

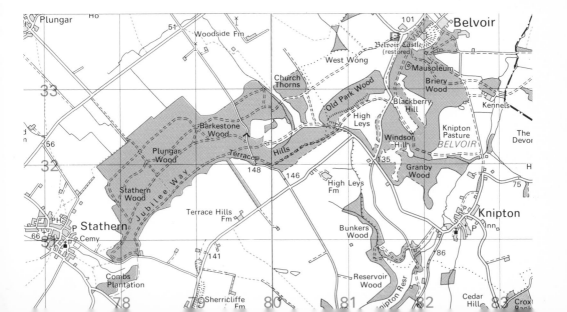

47 48
41 **42** 43
35 36 37

CENTRAL ENGLAND
South-West Lincolnshire and
the Soke Landranger sheets 131, 142

North-west of Peterborough the country is very quiet away from the A roads: oaks are thick and full leaved, ashes rather decorative as in eighteenth-century landscape painting. The soil is limy and hedges contain dog rose, maple and buckthorn. The cereal crops are tall. Endless vistas of electric pylons appear across the fields.

Southey Wood *109 025, (♀)⚲, 3 way-marked walks, $\frac{1}{2}$–$1\frac{1}{2}$m, FC*
The picnic and parking place is pleasant and clean and surrounded by tall Corsican pines and equally tall birches, and oaks. The woodlands are a series of compartments put together like Scrabble cards, mostly newly planted with various conifers.

A native wood towards Helpston is of oak (large, apparently hybrid), ash, maple and hazel; ash predominating. The atmosphere is soft and the colour a uniform greeny brown; the ground cover is of bramble, ground elder, nettles and plastic bags. Pheasants are reared.

Helpston *122 056*
This is John Clare's countryside. He was born and died (at seventy-one in 1875) in Helpston, the 'peasant poet' who, apart from a period in a lunatic asylum, lived here. He described the English countryside as no other poet has. His life spanned the decline of the old country of large heaths, grazed over, with picturesque small woods and streams. He ranted at the Inclosures. Now there is little he would recognize: his birthplace whitewashed, the heath devoted to crops, conifers, gravel-digging and rubbish disposal, in that order. Worst of all, his village, the centre of his universe in a network of heathland pathways and rural lanes, is now merely a collection of houses and a church at a crossroads on the B1443.

There *is* a stone monument in Helpston, apparently designed by the local pastrycook, and it carries the following verse, as if Clare had written his own epitaph:

The bard his glory ne'er receives,
Where summer's common flowers are
seen.

Dog rose in Bourne Wood

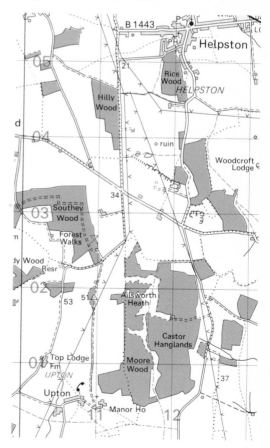

The Forestry Commission's Southey Wood

Campions in a Helpston hedge

But winter finds it when she leaves
The laurel only green
And time from that eternal tree
Shall weave a wreath to honour thee.

White campions, elder and dog rose in the
hedges are his best memorial.

A mile down Heath Road is a large grassy
parking place which has a few native trees and
has been planted with more, including
whitebeam, a tree which local authorities
always seem to have a lot of. Another mile
further south brings you to a common, *123
024*, called, for some reason, **Castor
Hanglands** (Castor is the next village), which
has been a National Nature Reserve since
1945. There has been time for a wilderness to
develop around the grassland, where rare
butterflies breed. There are large hawthorns,
very twisted, and biggish blackthorns amongst
the ash and oak. You are not encouraged to
enter. I don't think Clare would have
recognized this either. The common he knew
would be a fine, open place – though with
secret corners.

An ancient thorn in Castor Hanglands

Bourne Wood *077 201, ♀ ♠, 700 acres,
easy rides and paths, no waymarked walk,
FC*
The small-leaved lime was supposed to be
here, but I could not find it in this part of the
woods. There are, however, fine young
Huntingdon elms near the parking place
(which is large and open) and other elms
within. Good-quality ash and larch are being
taken out, Corsican pine put in, but there are
plenty of native trees left and some *Populus ×
euramericana*. This is a nice, workmanlike
wood, noisy with saws and smelling of larch
logs. There are miles of woodland that I could
not explore.

Huntingdon elms, Bourne Wood

Forest road, Bourne Wood

Marsh orchid, Callan's Lane

Callan's Lane Wood, Kirkby Underwood *060 270,* ♀ ♣ *, 300 acres, 3 forest walks, FC*

There is a picnic place but cars have to stay outside. The wood is a spruce and Douglas fir plantation with some Lawson cypress, western hemlock and noble fir. A Lawson cypress stands by the gate. The walk, marked blue with red or white for shorter routes, wanders amongst a wonderful variety of native trees, surfacing intermittently onto the forest road. The full-length walk is a longish trail, but you are rewarded with small-leaved lime, aspen, and a bit of beechwood with, in June, three sorts of orchid. The lime is an old coppice and two large stools had been cut recently. The route is clearly marked with sensible painted stobs which cannot be read backwards. The surrounding fields appear now and then, the

Callan's Lane Wood

Lincolnshire oaks, Mareham Lane, Willoughby

corn like a sea beating against the walls of the wood. Ash is dominant if you ignore the conifers, which *are* nicely integrated with the pattern.

You need wellingtons, and in an ordinary English summer a wet-suit as well, for the grass is long.

Woods are rare about Sleaford and apparently unknown around Boston. Trees are not absent however, and indeed are often impressively tall even though the map suggests a desert. At Aswarby are very fine parkland and roadside trees. Aswarby Thorns is an oak-ash wood with hawthorn underwood, blackthorn at the edges, and is more or less impenetrable even if access were allowed. Willoughby Gorse wood, a smaller wood on

the opposite side of the (Roman) road, *085 424*, Mareham Lane, is an oakwood partly converted to pine and can be walked in, outside the shooting season. The name Willoughby Gorse, coupled with Aswarby Thorns, indicates the character of the country before it was brought under the plough. The great water dock, not now a common plant in our well-drained countryside, is a feature of the ditches.

Thetford Forest, Section 37, extends to a large but comparatively young series of plantations west and south-west of Swaffham and there is a Forestry Commission picnic site on the A1122 – **Swaffham Heath**, *775 098*. This is the name only of what was once a very large heathland. A network of small sandy roads at the south-west side provides unofficial access to the pinewoods, which are especially attractive where there is a no-man's land of heath and grass between fields and forest. Lines of wind-blown, distorted Scots pines along the roads remind us of the pre-afforestation scenery.

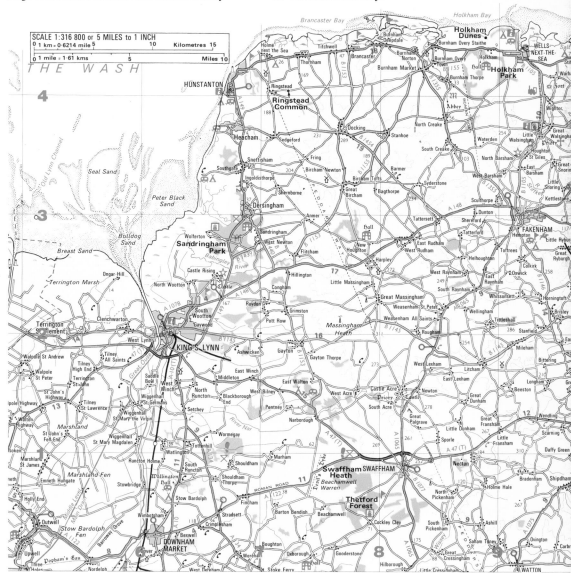

The Scottish Belt at Sandringham

Sandringham Park *695 286*; visited by millions and not short on tourist amenities, Sandringham is still effectively a nature reserve. A little ungratefully, I must report that the many very nice car parks seem to be taking over the space. Probably greater familiarity will enable one to trace more favourable routes. For a really easy short walk, the Scottish Belt, planted perhaps as a bit of Balmoral, which runs parallel to the main roadway with its wide verges, can be recommended. Dogs, naturally, are not discouraged, and children can have a whale of a time in the bracken or take the nature trail seriously without much danger of getting lost – there's always someone about.

Ringstead Common *727 405*, ♀ ♣ Inland from Hunstanton is the superbly brown and grey-patterned village of Ringstead. Take the narrow road to Burnham Market and stop at the first cross track for the Ringstead Charity Lands, where walkers are welcomed by a discreet notice. A mile of narrow but rather amazing woodland on the ridge to the north is planted like a wild arboretum, and crossed and

Sandringham, and a nearly cloudless afternoon

recrossed by mown green paths. The scrubland of the common is an interesting mixture of hawthorn and gorse.

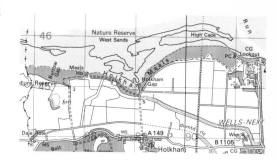

Holkham is beyond the Burnhams near Wells-next-the-Sea; it may attract you into its Park, *892 435*, on weekdays or, as it is closed at the weekends, you may choose to walk along the path of a Roman road for 2 miles beside a monumental brick-and-flint wall enclosing the estate. Start from the Burnham Thorpe to Wighton road at *862 400*. The woodland is of mature beech bordered by ilex; invaded by sycamore where not so mature. On reaching the coast road you can turn right and at the police notice saying 'No Parking' continue to the sea coast. Here the sand dunes are wooded with Corsican pine for 2 miles to the silted entrance of Wells Harbour. This is a most

untypical British wood, but refreshing – and a perfect playground for the caravanners on the large site behind the sea-wall at Wells-next-the-Sea. Here also is a large car park where I hope you will be met after your 5-mile tramp; walking back would be much less exciting.

No less than 9763 acres of, mostly, mud on the coast are a National Nature Reserve.

Ringstead Common: a slight sea-mist

North-East Norfolk

43 **44**
37 38

Landranger sheet 133

Sheringham – West Runton – Cromer

The steep Norfolk Heights above Cromer are well wooded and **Felbrigg Great Wood**, *204 403*, is an old oakwood. West Runton has a 70-acre section under National Trust care.
Roman Camp, here, *186 413*, is the name of the highest point in Norfolk, which of course is not saying much (329 feet). There is a pleasant, informal parking place near a caravan site (which is not intrusive and has a useful café) at **Beacon Hill**, *185 415*. The woods are superficially pretty but a little dusty and frayed, being too much frequented. Walking is directionless because of the many paths, but the very steep hillside guides our steps.

Sheringham Park, *140 420*, said to be Repton's masterpiece, seemed to be remarkable for the number of semi-tame pheasants among the heavy shrub layer of rhododendron. The park is open only in May and June. Working west there is Upper Sheringham Woodlands Caravan Park, and then Kelling Heath Caravan Site, almost a town amongst the birches and very much to be avoided – unless of course you occupy a van. One was named 'Bees Nees'. I was impressed by the well-organized services on the site.

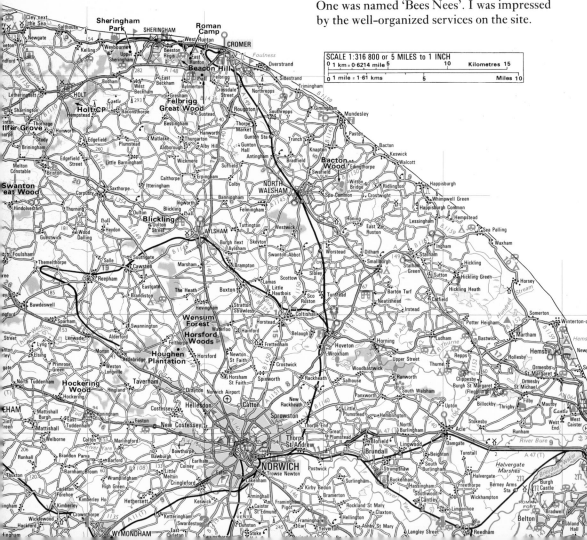

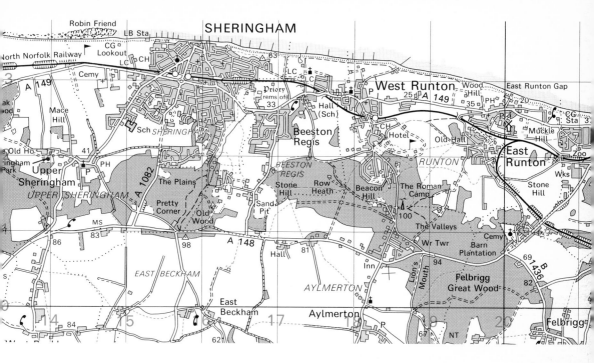

To get away from all that, 25 miles of the north Norfolk coast are protected by reserves. Try Blakeney Point, a long shingle walk from Cley-next-the-Sea or by boat from Blakeney. You will not see a single caravan, nor a tree.

Holt Country Park *083 370*, ♀ ♣, *various routes mapped, CP*
Holt is inland: a boom town but nice. Just outside the town on the Norwich road, the B1149, the Country Park is signposted from the new bypass. This is an old estate with curious sculptures; although there is much coniferous woodland there remain many gaps for a lush native vegetation to creep in. It is especially attractive towards the Hempstead road. Beyond this road there is a belt of mature pine some 2 miles long with softly overgrown rides; a lonely place.

Swanton Novers, further inland, is an ordinary small village under a great mass of tall trees. Swanton Great Wood, *020 315*, is a nature reserve where small-leaved lime is abundant, and it is remarkable for many ancient coppice stools, one measuring 27 feet

across. There are 50 acres of coppiced oak, and patches where sessile oak and lime share the ground, along with native bird cherry, *Prunus padus*. The May lily, a rare woodland plant, may be native here. There is a plateau alderwood here on some of the highest ground in Norfolk, with fen carr below.

Bullfer Grove *017 359*, ♀ ♣, *8 acres, NT*
North of Gunthorpe off the A148, this small wood makes a very short walk. The wood surrounds an old quarry. Its chief attraction appears to be its edges, particularly along the lovely deep, oak-lined lane.

Blickling Hall, *178 286*, one of the very finest National Trust properties, is in a well-wooded valley and the parkland is always open. There is a great oriental plane, forming a wood on its own, and other exotic trees including magnolias. The Jacobean house is approached between 15-foot-wide yew hedges.

North of Norwich are the scattered pieces of what the Forestry Commission calls **Wensum Forest**; perhaps the pieces will one day join together. Nearest the sea is **Bacton Wood,** *317*

312, locally known as Witton Wood; once it was Witton Heath, with ancient oaks. Here are now no less than thirty different forestry trees. The Forestry Commission has exploited a varied sandy soil to combine timber production with deliberately attractive planting. Following the prescribed walk, you will encounter native birch and beech, Corsican pine, then western hemlock, sweet chestnut, Douglas fir, grand fir, Scots pine, hybrid larch, and the western red cedar, *Thuja plicata*, from western Canada and north USA.

In the valley are a beautiful silver fir, *Abies concolor*, Norway spruce, Lawson's cypress and more *Thuja*; oak – a very old one – English cherry, a lime avenue-to-be, and, as you return, an ornamental belt including the American red oak with its large spiky leaves, and Norway maple, also spiky leaved and smooth barked. A leaflet guide is available from the Forestry Commission at Santon Downham.

About the large patches of green on the map approximately 5 miles north of Norwich there is less to be said. As far as I can see the best walks are from the north end of St Helens (off the B1149), through the attractive deciduous woodland of **Houghen Plantation**, *187 172*, to Felthorpe Church – you can return by a different route. A little further north at the crossroads a wide ride leads off north-east through **Horsford Woods** – conifers in straight lines, but you *can* step out. The Forest Office is at Newton St Faith, to the east of the A140 to Cromer, but as yet it is not a public information office. For the rest, private property development has spoiled the old unities of land and villages and laced the woodlands with eyesores and fences.

South of Norwich, and not easy to find, at *172 004* is the **Hethel Thorn**, or Witch of Hethel, a nature reserve consisting of one tree. It may have been planted in the reign of King John, but it is more likely that it just grew there. There is no record of anyone planting any tree at that period of history (AD 1200). Before it was made into a nature reserve someone unkindly cut it down, so it is only the witch's sucker shoots that you see now.

At the western edge of the Wensum Forest complex, near East Dereham on the A47(T) is Hockering. Turn off north, 1 mile, for **Hockering Wood**, *072 150*, an ancient stronghold of the small-leaved lime, *Tilia cordata*: about 200 acres.

The path by Bullfer Grove

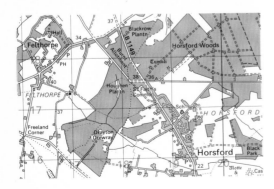

North Cheshire and the Wirral

Landranger sheets 108, 109, 117, 118

THE CHESHIRE PLAIN

Cheshire has three per cent of its land under woodland, only half the national average, and the woods are hard to see as you drive over the wide, softly undulating plain which is filled with heavy, rather small trees – oaks and sycamores – and smells of cow dung and nettles. Clay overlies a sheet of rust-coloured limestone through which sandstone outcrops dramatically, particularly at the Delamere Forest, or what remains of it.

Delamere Forest *556 704 (Delamere Railway Station), (♀) ♣, 2m by 1m. Forest walks and trail, FC*
There are 2000 acres of trees here, half of all Cheshire's Scots pines (800 acres) and nearly all her Corsican pines (600 acres). That leaves 600 acres to be made up mainly of larch,

spruce, oak and birch. On the ground, the pines seem very much to dominate, with narrow strips of pretty oak-birch woodland along the two roads which cross the forest (meeting at Hatchmere). The Sandstone Trail,

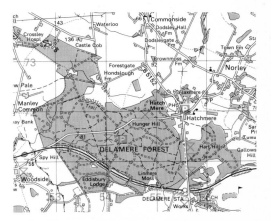

Roadside woodland in Delamere Forest – perhaps the original vegetation

Seedling oak in the heather, Little Budworth
Common

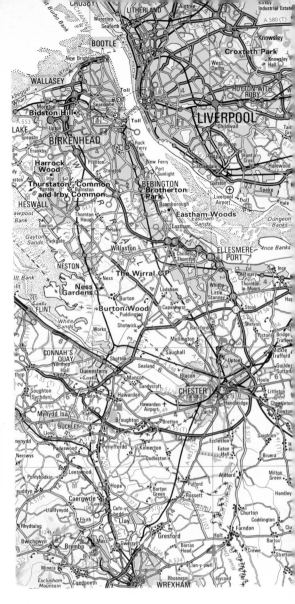

14 miles long, passes through the forest. The part of it I tried to follow was not marked at a crucial junction and I found myself back on the road. The pinewoods are full of the sour smells of fox and bracken and the monotony is broken only by an occasional bog full of rushes, or an elder tree seeming exotically perfumed here, or a great clearing splendidly sprouting millions of foxgloves. But the path lives up to its name of Sandstone, and you could pad along in silence for two hours through the trees, if you could be sure of the way.

There are four Forestry Commission walks, some linking up with the trail, and three picnic areas, two with WCs (actually Portaloos). The road running west from Hatchmere (where water-lilies spread and caravans cluster) is the prettier, but has parking bays all the way along, ready, one feels, for the thoughtless crowds on bank holidays. Rather wider margins of hardwoods would have seemed a bit less cynically production-minded. There is a pleasant grassy picnic place arranged by the local authority at the end of the road just beyond the forest, at Woodside, *523 707*: clean grass with a few willows augmented by planting.

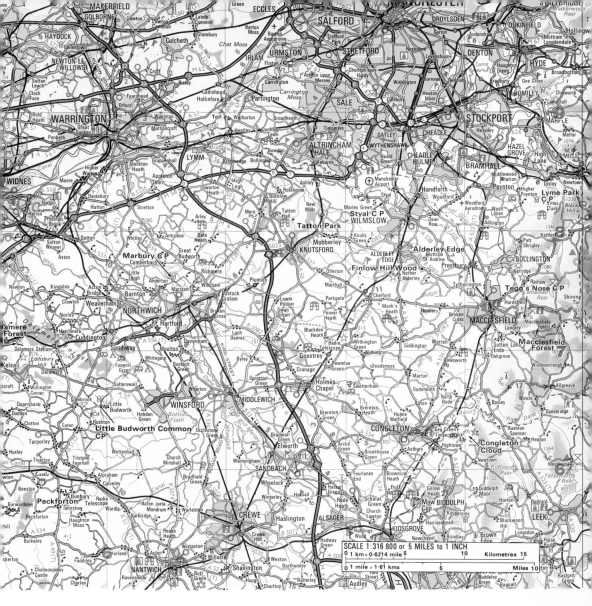

Little Budworth Common 583 663, ☿, 200 acres, CP

This is a large birch common of loose sand covered by dull ling – and a few spots of purple heather. You could be anywhere. But thank goodness the Forestry Commission didn't get its hands on it. Oak seems to be spreading; perhaps in time it will take over and make a really nice wood. Parking places are unpretentious. Motor racing occurs at Oulton Park, adjacent to the south. The Marbury Country Park, more secluded, would be a better choice for a day out.

Budworth Mere, 8 miles away on the other side of Northwich, is a famous wildfowl refuge with the nature reserve of Marbury Reed Beds, 14 acres, fenced off. The mere is now part of **Marbury Country Park**, 190 acres, 649 763. There is scattered woodland in the park. The many meres of this area are the result of subsidence following deliberate flooding to pump out rock salt. The salt seams, sometimes 100 feet thick, resulted from the evaporation of the seas which laid down the Red Marl itself. How long does it take to deposit 100 feet of salt by evaporation, I wonder?

91

Tatton Park, National Trust, is now a
Country Park of 988 acres, parkland, open to
pedestrians, free, from 9 o'clock daily; *748 827*
and other entrances. Rostherne, to the north, is
a village of poetic beauty, the church
fascinatingly out of perspective and black,
perched high over the mere, which is a
National Nature Reserve and said to be the
finest mere. There are many trees.

THE WIRRAL

One of the first Country Parks was that of the
Wirral. It is linear, following an old railway
from Hooton to West Kirby, through thick and
thin, suburb, farm and town, emerging onto
the sea-wall at *273 790*, north of Neston, to
confront an amazing 'sea' of grass and rushes.
This trail is only occasionally wooded. Various
shaded picnic places are along the route;
information at Thurstaston, *236 835*. Hadlow
Road Railway Station, Willaston, is preserved
in its original state.

Thurstaston Common and **Irby
Common** *244 846*, ♀ ♣ *(Scots pines),
about 200 acres, many paths, NT*
The Wirral proves unexpectedly bony here,
with exquisite stratification of the sandstone
revealed where the A540 cuts through the hill
near the car park. Thurstaston Common is
mainly heather, but has a fringe of beautiful
birch-pine woodland, the pines to the east
widely spaced, tall and uncluttered. A wooded
pathway leads from the south-east corner (at
the end of Sandy Lane – there is space to park)
up to the much smaller Irby Common, a
birchwood. Here gorse is dying and oak
coming up with lovely hair grass.

The sandstone surfaces again at **Bidston
Hill**, *293 892*, in suburban Birkenhead. You
can certainly walk across to the windmill (via a
footbridge over a road which cuts through the
common) but there seems to be nowhere
special to park a car.

> From Blacon Point to Hilbree
> A squirrel may leap from tree to tree.

Blacon is near Chester and Hilbree is the
largest of three small tidal islands off West
Kirby – no place for squirrels now, but a
nature reserve for seals and oyster catchers.

Peckforton *540 575 (access point)*, ♀,
steepish fp, pf
South of Beeston Castle, which is on another of

Delamere Forest

those sandstone knobs, is a 3-mile escarpment covered thickly with oakwoods. These are private, but the Sandstone Way runs along the west side, and there is a feeder path across the hill, through the oaks. On the minor road from Beeston to Peckforton look for the massive Victorian, baronial lodge gates; at the left, where you can scarcely see it if you are not looking for it, is a footpath sign. You are expected, and frequently reminded, to stick to the path. This is a 'conservation area', or, more accurately, a game preserve – many a pheasant pie is eaten in the name of conservation. The woods are extremely natural-looking, and they

93

are full of bracken with patches of bilberry: probably the best oakwoods in Cheshire. A dead birch is completely covered in orange-yellow bracket fungus, and looks like a hitherto unknown species of tree. Fifteen minutes uphill and five down on the other side bring you to the Sandstone Way – north to Beeston, south to Bulkeley Hill, straight on to Tattenhall Lane and Burwardsley. A black and white cottage with small-paned windows and octagonal chimneys sits demurely on a heathland of rounded bushes patrolled by game birds.

At Nantwich, a most attractive town with many half-timbered old houses and a fine sandstone church, is the new (1972) **Granada Arboretum** of Manchester University. It is open only seasonally at present.

Ness Gardens *305 756*, ♀ ♣ , *¾m round, Liverpool University*

Small but stunningly well looked after, the gardens have benefited from well-established patches of shelter-belt woodland to the south-west and the north-east, and there are many young and mature trees of interest as well. There are well-contrasted groups of Lawson cypress cultivars, a pinewood 200 yards long, good blue spruce, Delavey's fir, Italian alder, a fine heather garden, a 'spinney' of spaced-out beeches, a magnificent rock garden with a rich

Summer sunlight on Irby Common

Ness Gardens, Wirral

pattern of small and dwarf conifers contrasted with a tall, yew hedge. The wide Dee Estuary is glimpsed beyond. There are few labels on the trees, but herbaceous plants are thoroughly labelled: there is a herb garden including aromatic plants with braille labels. There is a reading room and a Visitors' Centre.

At **Burton**, a handsome village 1 mile to the south, is a small (20-acre) wood, of old oak augmented with tall pines, belonging to the National Trust. There *is* space to park at the north-east side of the wood, *315 747*, but the road should not be attempted with an ordinary car (though it may now be repaired).

On the Mersey side of the Wirral, **Eastham**

Thurstaston Common

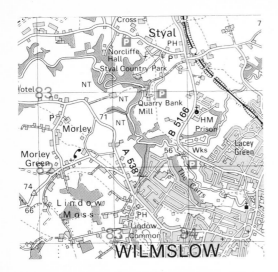

Woods, *363 820*, are a 27-acre Country Park. Between Eastham village and Bebington is the Dibbin Brook, with rather occluded ancient woodland in a local nature reserve, **Brotherton Park**. The National Trust has a 10-acre piece, **Harrock Wood**, *263 846*. Across the water, only $3\frac{1}{2}$ miles from the Liver Building, is Liverpool's **Croxteth Park**, now Country Park, 500 acres, *399 943*: hall, old orchard and walled garden, parkland and woodland, even forestry.

Styal *835 830 Northern Woods and Mill, 840 821 Southern Woods*, ♀ ♠ , *252 acres, riverside walks, NT, CP*

Only 8 miles from Piccadilly, Manchester, as the magpie flies (they are now more common and visible than crows) are impressive tall beeches, larches, and one *Sequoiadendron* left over from a group which must have got too tall for comfort. These are in the Northern Wood: picturesque, but eroded by too many feet – and the River Bollin *smells*. Worse, the noise of jet take-off from Manchester Airport is quite killing.

Further upstream the Southern Woods are quieter, occasionally weird, still smelly, and full of policeman's helmet (Himalayan balsam). Beech and pine level out to willow and, of all things, hornbeam, towards the meadows and Wilmslow. I like to think the hornbeams – one is a reasonably old coppice tree – were planted to provide teeth for the cogs of the mill around which this plantation is orientated. The mill, 1784, and the village which grew around it under the enterprise and care of one mill owner are all a National Trust property of 252 acres.

Alderley Edge *860 773*, ♀ ♠ *(Scots pines), 200 acres, many paths, wheelchair route, NT*

Poor old Alderley Edge, famous as a beauty-spot to many Mancunians long before 1947 when it came to the National Trust: dug into by miners from the Stone Age to the nineteenth century, then privately owned and loved, planted with pines and beeches (over natural birch and oak); and now with erosion and litter problems. The view through a delicate lattice of beech boughs to a wide

countryside heavy with trees, cows and nice detached houses, is still attractive: Black Hill and Shining Tor to the east. There is a large parking place near The Wizard (pub, now a restaurant, National Trust). A wheelchair path circumnavigates the woodlands, which can still be enchanting, like a lovely melody on a scratchy old record. So many people have loved this place: one American even donated a brass plate to mark the site of a beacon fire. A footpath from the Alderley road (at the west end) is signposted in native cast iron: 'To the Edge'. The names of the Misses Pilkington, who gave the acres to the nation, are engraved on a rock.

A nice wood is across the Macclesfield road and south: **Finlow Hill Wood**, *856 766*. It is a

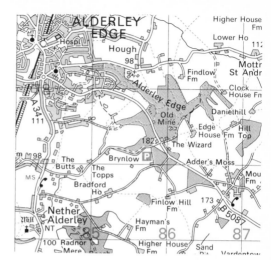

Alderley Edge, early morning (slight drizzle)

small birchwood, once coppiced, with young oaks coming up, pretty and straightforward. The floor is covered with hair grass, bedstraw and white-flowered, not too vigorous, *Rubus*. Alarmingly dense patches of bracken are on the march: I wish someone would cut them.

Macclesfield Forest *975 722 (village)*, ♀, *100 acres, roads through, WA*

The lovely smooth green mantle on the hills south-east of Macclesfield is perhaps best viewed with its reflection in the still waters of Ridgegate Reservoir above Langley, or from the heights of **Tegg's Nose Country Park**, *950 723*. The great plantation makes visual sense and other sorts of sense, but I did not try any of the walks. Macclesfield Forest was probably a treeless moorland for hunting the wild boar, with wild woods in the cloughs. Now it is a catchment area with a large plantation of conifers.

Tegg's Nose summit is on the Gritstone Trail, a long-distance path. The Forest Chapel is the next stop. The old hilltop quarry is not the worst place to spend a wet Monday morning, and should be exciting on a fine day,

The path to Tegg's Nose summit, lined with heather and sallow, with a view to the Macclesfied Forest

with its bird's-eye view of the surrounding hill pastures, reservoir, roads, the great forest and the skyline of tors. The quarry workings are covered attractively by heather and sallows, and are scattered with preserved relics of the stone-workers. Gritstone, we are told, is easy to work when first quarried. Glass-covered panels explain the geology and its exploitation, in a gritstone shelter, with gritstone blocks cemented to the ground outside. It looks fairly hard stuff – and touchingly familiar to one whose childhood was 4 feet closer to similar drains, kerbs and setts. These silent blocks of

stone and half-dismembered machines in the rain are a strange memorial perhaps to the generation of craftsmanship and sweat; but better than an empty hole in the hill, however prettily overgrown. Quarrying ceased in 1955.

Lyme Park (*965 844* for the Country Park, or walk in at any of several points around the 1300 acres) is one of the greatest houses – Palladian façade but looking rather as if transported from central Liverpool. The park is high, up to 1220 feet, and 9 miles round. There are an inner and an outer perambulation, and, for those with what it takes, the Gritstone Trail goes south to Tegg's Nose.

Guides for the Gritstone Trail, the Sandstone Trail, and also for the shorter Mow Cop Trail and The Whitegate Way, a disused railway near Sandigate, are available from the Tourist Office at the Town Hall, Chester CH1 1SF.

And so to the clouds. Congleton has a Cloud, *903 636* National Trust, and there are others – overleaf.

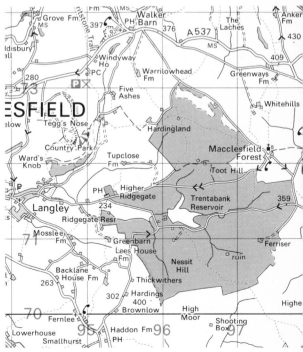

The Peak District

Landranger sheets 110, 119

The Peak District is an upland, not a woodland area, and only dimly remembers being a forest. The woods are in the deeply cut valleys or on moorland reclaimed for forestry. Looking at just the woods may seem to belittle the National Park: this is not intended. Quite a lot of the woods, anyway, are outside the boundary of the Park to the east. I have drawn a line north and south through Bakewell only for convenience.

Masonry and railways are out of fashion now, while concrete and roads are in. The Peak District's Carboniferous rocks are largely of limestone, held in a trough or anticline of gritstone, which sticks out at the edges in well-known scarps. The Millstone Grit is now neglected, but the limestone is more and more in demand. The creation of the National Park certainly saved the lovely green hills from being smashed to bits. Look at the Hind Low arm of the Buxton 'island' in the Park: devastating! In return we have a fine disused railway walk and deserted gritstone quarries, as at Tegg's Nose – in the Park but in our previous section.

The farmland of the southern or 'White' Peak is too rich to be wasted on mere trees, but much of it remains green, not ploughed, with gleaming white drystone walls protecting the rich wayside flora of the Mountain Limestone. The National Park is ringed by great industrial conurbations and the beauty-spots are under pressure. To south-easterners it is way up north; they should come and see, but, as I am careful to say, avoid the best-known dales at holiday times. I love the rich fruit-cake patterns of the towns and the proud energy of the industries and quarries as much as the woods and fields (but I can't stand the A6). Anyway, country and industry are usually better kept separate, which is what National Parks are for.

WEST OF BAKEWELL

The Roaches *005 621,* ✦ ✹*, ½m to 2m and back, fps*
Hen Cloud, with gritstone feathers raised to the winds, the Roaches, and the Five Clouds below them – five chicks really – are strangely shaped and weathered outcrops overlooking the Cheshire Plain. You can walk over the top of the Roaches and then back through mostly dying larchwoods below, keeping an eye out for wallabies, resident since evacuated in World War II to a nearby zoo. At weekends climbers, traditionally shouting loudly and continuously, practise short pitches on the rocks. Patches of dead larchwood are extravagantly beautiful, a petrified forest of elegant skeletons.

Cranesbill and limestone wall in the White Peak

Goyt Woodlands *013 757*, 👤 🏕 ,
1½m trail, 3m long wooded valley, FC
These woods on the west side of the Fernilee
and Errwood Reservoirs are reached by
turning off the A5002 north of Buxton at the
signpost to Goyt Valley. The narrow road,
which turns south along the reservoir and then
climbs out along the moors to the Cat and
Fiddle Pass (A54) is now one-way and is closed
to traffic on Sundays and bank holidays. The
map reference is for the disabled car park by
the water. There are several parking places in
the woodland along the road. If you want to
park in shade you have to take your choice

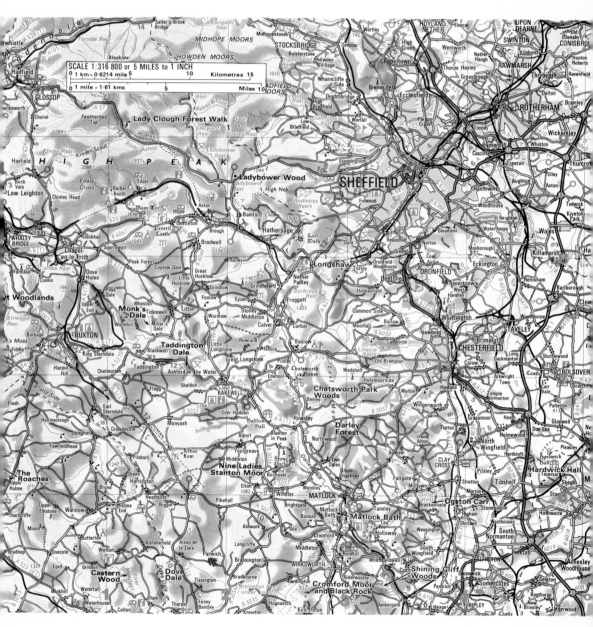

before reaching the attractive but exposed quarry car park, *012 732*, at the southern or upper end of the woodland.

Large, impressive larches, Scottish-looking pines and big beeches are mingled with the native oaks, rowans and birches above the stony River Goyt: smooth moorlands beyond are planted with the Commission's pines, at well above what appears to be the natural tree-line. A wide, easy path follows the stream as the trees become fewer: but at a final picnic place at Derbyshire Bridge, *018 716*, well onto the moors, a large wych elm, perfectly healthy, shows just what trees can do. The Goyt Valley, with its reservoirs, is a sometimes gloomy, always impressive area with beautiful woodlands.

From Ashbourne to Buxton is a favourite road, the A515, which takes you smoothly through green hills and white walls out of the sleepy (except for lorries) Midlands town of Ashbourne to the North, here symbolized by the Edwardian opulence of Buxton, overlaid by cheerful, modern vulgarity but still producing good pork pies. Turn off for Dove Dale – or avoid it at busy times.

Dove Dale *north from 147 509, ♀, 854 acres, NT; several adjoining properties, woods and valleys, easy riverside walk, 2–8m (very steep valley sides), nature trail from Ilam CP*

The valley is heavily wooded but far too famous: claustrophobic, hot and busy in summer, at least as far up as Milldale. The Country Park at Ilam is gracious but I thought the Manifold looked dirty and the Dove at Milldale not much better. Avoiding the crowds on a hot July Monday (what could it be like on a Sunday?), I tramped across the Ilam Tops between little woods of sycamore to look down the valley. The view of Tissington Spires and Thorpe Cloud was impressive. A footpath from Air Cottage at the Tops descends through the woods, which are heavily invaded by sycamore from the upland shelter-belts. Ash is the native dominant.

Castern Wood, *121 538*, is a 55-acre nature reserve in the Manifold Valley, with a great diversity of trees and shrubs.

Besides Dove Dale and the Manifold Valley there are, near Bakewell, Miller's Dale and Ravensdale, Deep Dale and Monsal Dale, and, recommended as an alternative, **Lathkill Dale**, 3 miles, wooded, east and down from *175 655* to Over Haddon, *205 665*, where one can park. Part of the dale is a National Nature Reserve; with **Monk's Dale** to the north-west, *141 725*, a total of 650 acres. Monk's Dale has an unspoilt range of habitat from woodland,

In the Goyt Valley

scrub and grass to marsh and bare rock. Cheedale, *124 736*, has a 60-acre reserve of the Derbyshire Naturalists' Trust. A permit is needed for this and other woodlands of the Trust, including the large Miller's Dale woodlands below them. **Taddington Dale**, *165 708*, has 60 acres of National Trust woodland, but it also has the A6(T).

The High Peak Trail, following an old railway (especially from Sparklow, *127 659*, where there is a pleasant parking place, south to Parsley Hay), offers excellent non-woodland scenery in this most beautiful of all high pasture.

EAST OF BAKEWELL

Darley Forest *293 655, (♀)♠, 1200 acres, roads and rides, FC*
Come here if you can, there's plenty of room. The air is intoxicating, the dew in the morning sunlight like blue and yellow crystals – believe it or not. The rows and rows of pines are saturnine; birches and rowans line the roads, where the drystone walls, set well back, give plenty of room for cars to stop. Buttercups and clover line the verges with patches of bedstraw, milkwort and tormentil. It doesn't matter where you walk, and there is no nonsense

Dove Dale

The road through the Darley Forest

about picnic places. While I ate my breakfast I talked to a man old enough to be my father, who walked 4 or 5 miles in the forest every morning on a cup of tea. He said he wasn't very well.

Nine Ladies, Stanton Moor *253 630*, ♀, *2m, fps, NT*

The Nine Ladies above Darley Dale are the stones of a not very impressive henge, looking more like well-worn teeth than ladies and surrounded by a protective wall which must surely damp any vibrations for those sensitive to such things. The stone circle is in a wood.

Henges, at first wood henges, were I believe a diagrammatic representation of the ancestral woodland home, built on land cleared for grazing. This is just a theory of mine – but why should the people bury wood charcoal under the main stones unless it was the sacred earth of the woodland? The woodland here is of birch, partly old coppice and partly burned. I don't know whether the National Trust knows its birchwood is being burned. The remains of this birch coppice high on the moors are interesting, I don't know quite why. There are many old quarries with rowan and birch spreading, one quarry working.

Darley Moor and Darley Forest

The view from Black Rock on the High Peak Trail

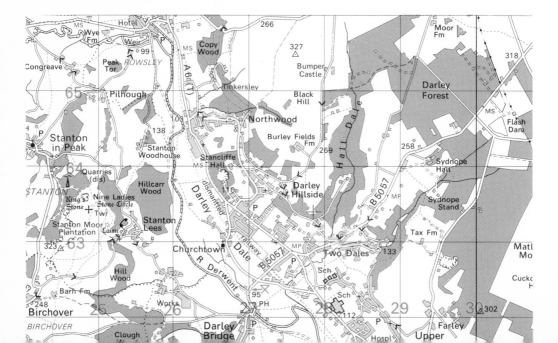

At **Matlock Bath**, *290 585*, there are trees
to walk in, actually advertised as Lovers'
Walks, and you have only to cross the valley
road for a bag of chips.

Via Gellia, west from Cromford, is a drive
on the A5012 through a heavily wooded valley
(not a street of ice-cream vendors as the name
might suggest). A fine dust of limestone is
deposited in dry weather.

Cromford Moor and **Black Rock** *291
557*, (♀)♣, *waymarked walks, FC, CC*
These black rocks south of Matlock are of
Millstone Grit, only black by contrast with the
limestone of the 'White Peak' – both are visible
here. Elsewhere, black basalt 'toad stones'
surface above the limestone. The picnic place
is in a moderately built-up area and opposite a
busy quarry which is noisy on weekdays. On

fine Sundays the very capacious car park, on
several terraces of the hillside, is full of people
sunbathing on the banks while the children
climb the rocks.

The High Peak Trail, sensibly waymarked
with numbered posts, passes here (post
number 6) before descending to the narrow
valley of the Derwent/A6/Cromford Canal.

In the large, ragged-outlined plantation east
and south of the rocks are the Forestry
Commission's 300 acres of vigorous young
Scots pines, with some Corsican pine at the
edges and pretty western hemlocks by the
trail. The rides or firebreaks avoid monotony
on the uneven ground and are full of native
plants. But note that the rides run roughly
parallel to the path at the cliff edge; do not
imagine that following one of them will bring
you back to the parking place. The atmosphere
is wild and remote in spite of the proximity of
roads and industry, for the plantation covers a
shallow bowl on the hilltop, strangely out of
contact with the surroundings.

Chatsworth Park Woods *271 685*, ♀ (♣),
3½m plus return or as you choose, pf
Parking at the house is reasonable, but you
may be too early, or wish to avoid the crush on
a fine holiday. The map reference is for Beeley
Hilltop Farm where you can pick up a yellow-
arrowed footpath northwards (signed to Robin
Hood). After 15 minutes of an easy gradient on
the bracken moor – a few boggy patches – you
join a sandy roadway which enters the estate
woodlands. These are of mature beech with
infillings of pine and infiltrations of sycamore;
some old yews near the house. Rhododendron
is much in evidence. There are several more or
less parallel routes signalled by lilac or white
arrows, the lower paths being walkways with
grotesque features as designed in the late
eighteenth century. The spectacular plumbing
arrangements – aqueducts of rustic stonework
– of the Chatsworth landscape can be viewed,
with longer views (in good weather, thrilling
ones) over the house and park and the
surrounding moors.

On a busy day you will be overtaken by
parties of old-age pensioners attired for hiking
and moving fast: to them the park is just an

Eighteenth-century waterworks above Chatsworth Park

incident, just a change of scenery. Walking is a very popular hobby in Derbyshire, almost a way of life. If you are a moderate walker like me and the day is fine, take food and allow a whole day for this picturesque place.

Longshaw *266 799, ♀ ♠, 1000 acres plus, network of paths, NT*

The parking ground given is among trees and you can walk north-westwards by the Sheffield Plantation. Much of this has been fenced off as newly planted, but it is now quite well grown and the fence could be removed. The mixture of pine and hardwoods will need thinning before it can be walked in, but the final result should be effective. A pleasant though rather thin wood of mature pine survives on grazing lands and marsh to the north. The shop, open at weekends, at Longshaw Lodge, can provide a leaflet, but, except to establish the main feature by a simplistic map, this tells one nothing. Grindleford Station will bring you from Manchester by train: you only have to cross the road. I can't imagine this strangely shapeless but attractive moorland-parkland

BELOW: trees at Longshaw

except on the perfect July day on which I saw it: full of happy people with a great mound of flowering rhododendrons and a moon-landscape of moors beyond. Dogs must be very well behaved because of the sheep.

The whole of the east bank of the Derwent southwards to Froggatt is wooded and belongs to the Trust as does the moorland edge above. To the north-west the Trust's land extends south of the A625 to within a mile of Hathersage.

In Derwentdale, to the north of the section close to Huddersfield, Sheffield and Glossop, are large Forestry Commission plantations around the great Derwent and Ladybower Reservoirs, with many parking and picnic places. The Forestry Commission lists the **Lady Clough Forest Walk** from a lay-by on the A57 at *110 915*, and recommends stout footwear.

Ladybower Wood, Bamford, *205 867*, (track east of Ladybower pub 1 mile on the A57) is a nature reserve, 40 acres of native trees. **Ogston Carr** and plantations, *372 596*,

Hardwick Hall, with a silver lime

also on the gritstone, form an 80-acre nature reserve.

The roads eastwards to Edwinstowe and Sherwood Forest are the A617 and the A6075.

Along the Derwent towards Belper the deep valley is clothed in trees: on the west bank are **Shining Cliff Woods**, National Trust leased to the Forestry Commission. These shine only in places and are difficult to get into from the valley, but National Trust ownership does at least ensure that no more houses will be built in the woodland. A broad arm extends westwards on the hilltop where, at *322 525*, you can just about park and then walk into the woods, here under young conifers; whitebeams along Jackass Lane (which may have been named after a male ass, but more likely refers to an idiot – I recognize the vernacular from my youth). From Ambergate or from Whatstandwell, in the valley, there are footpaths all the way through, but approached awkwardly through private settlements: and the woods are of little interest in themselves. Whatstandwell is not, apparently, Old Norse, but was named rather prosaically after one Walt Stonewell, many centuries ago, but there are many tree names in the farmland – not moorland – above the valley, notably Alderwasley: 'alder wash ley' – a wet alder pasture.

Hardwick Hall *436 638 and 453 640*, ♀ ♣ *(parkland), 250 acres, CP in 2000 acres, NT*

If you do not want to see the house, or its herb garden, drive through to the lower parking place, or the Hardwick pub. The grounds are freely open during daylight hours. The house, of course, is a real treasure, of stone lifted out of the nearby quarry and carved with elephantine elegance into the monogram E.S. (for Elizabeth Shrewsbury), which repeats over the flat façade – luxuriously fenestrated by Elizabethan standards – even by any standard. The windows now have a good view of the M1. The park is a bit plain, but compared with some of the landscape round about, it is Elysium: little actual woodland. There is a nature trail.

Sherwood Forest, Newark and Gainsborough
Landranger sheets 112, 120, 121

SHERWOOD FOREST

Sherwood has been described as a purely literary forest, and it is true that the 25 or so square miles of Scots and Corsican pines between Nottingham and Worksop are largely reconstituted from the chases, parks, coverts and warrens of the Dukeries. The dukes and earls, however, did not neglect to plant trees as well as mining coal: it was the demands of World Wars I and II that finally demolished the forest, which is on sandy ground where regeneration is not automatic. Heath with scattered birch is the result of clearing the oaks, at least for a century or so as the oaks gradually creep back into the maturing birch thickets. Mining has probably very much lowered the water table.

All is not lost however. Robin still lives, powerfully preserved by the Robin Hood Society, Mansfield, and in numerous Ladybird books and others sold at the Visitors' Centre, and in the propped-up limbs of the great Major Oak, visited by 200,000 people a year and piously believed to be Robin Hood's favourite tree. There is more: 450 acres here are claimed to be the oldest piece of ancient oak forest in western Europe.

Sherwood Forest CP, Edwinstowe
627 677, ♀, 500 acres, 5 walks, CC
There are a wheelchair path, 1 mile to the Major Oak, a blind trail with handrail, $\frac{3}{4}$ mile, and 3 other walks, the longest $4\frac{1}{2}$ miles. All start from the Visitors' Centre at Edwinstowe.

Go straight for the Centre, in spite of the 'tasteful' script lettering, actually very vulgar, and the often-repeated 'portrait' of Robin Hood. Collect the leaflet and get away. The longest walk is marked yellow and is arranged

The Major Oak, Sherwood Forest

by the Rotary Club of Sherwood Forest to take in a large, grassy heath used for Army training, which area the Rotary believes, I think rightly, to be typical of the original Sherwood Forest. I did this walk and whilst in the process was able to sample the other walks, bridleways and footpaths which join and cross. I also sampled the forest ride through the pines. I feel I saw enough large, dead oaks and scrubby birches to last me a long time, and I honestly think that if you don't want to walk far you can see everything worth seeing by combining the routes as below. Separate and quite short is the trail for the blind, with a tapping- or hand-rail

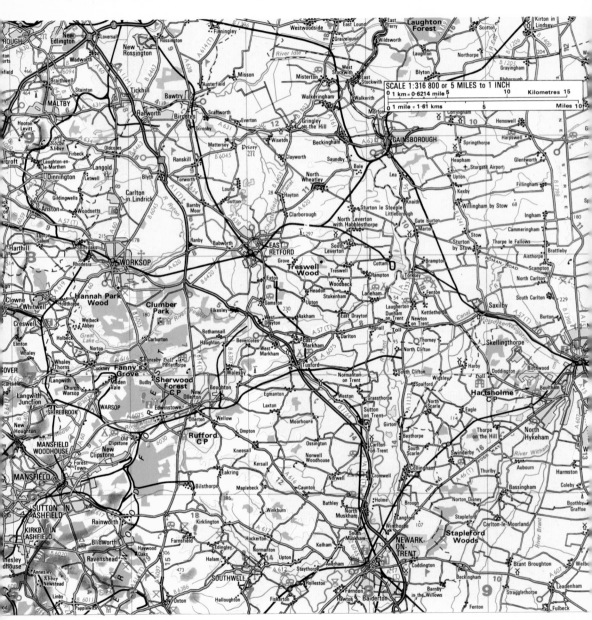

on the right all the way, and with patches of gravel to indicate features. The 'features' are pathetically limited, culminating in an opportunity to compare oak, yew and birch bark in the cool of a tiny yew wood. I tested the whole thing: bird song was magnificent, for the rest I felt very glad to have the sight of my eyes. I couldn't even smell the bracken. There is a lot of bracken here but the time is coming when we shall be able to make use of it according to research being done at the Institute of Terrestrial Ecology.

The walk: take the blind trail until you reach the start of the footpath signed To Budby Only – do not take this but turn left onto the blue-marked Major Oak path, which is wide and surfaced for wheelchairs. Follow this clockwise round the Major Oak and part of the way back until you see the green and yellow posts indicating a path to the left (actually northwards). A short way along this, opposite a stand of pines, is a remarkable oak stub, hemispherical, living, and about 8 feet in diameter. Fortunately no one has thought of

putting up a notice saying that Robin Hood used to cut his bow-stakes here, or the place would be trampled flat. Nevertheless that might be the case. The green route goes off left here and if followed a short way will give a view of the open heath. To the right is a lovely field of grass with a beautiful birchwood

An ancient coppiced oak in Sherwood Forest

In the trees, Sherwood Forest

Fanny's Grove, noisy but pretty, with good timber oaks

beyond. You could return this way by the Budby path, a total distance of about $1\frac{1}{2}$ miles.

Regeneration of the oak is quite vigorous, especially in areas which have been rabbit-fenced. Several of the large old trees are sessile or hybrid, but all the young trees I looked at were pedunculate. The pedunculate oak is said to have been encouraged. It does seem that its seed is more viable and adaptable to drought conditions. Many stag-headed old trees have almost certainly suffered from a reduction in their water supply too rapid for adaptation; obviously this is their way of adapting. I believe that most of the now-dead trees would have been in full leaf if the drainage pattern had not been changed.

RIGHT: Corsican pine thrusting up, and ancient oak dying back, Sherwood Forest

Open land in Sherwood Forest

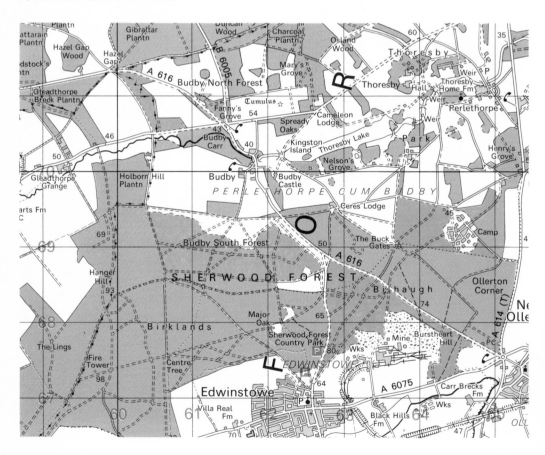

There are other parking places: at Rufford Country Park – lake, mill (converted), Abbey (or craft centre) and small wood, 182 acres, *646 656*, and another parking place about ½ mile south; also at **Fanny's Grove**, *612 709*, off the A616. The latter has a cruelly shadeless car park but the grove of well-grown oaks, about one in four sessile, is a splendid sight.

Clumber Park *645 773 (main entrance)*, ♀ ♣, *4000 acres, drives, walks, bicycle rides, nature trail, NT*
The house is gone, but the Capability Brown lake remains. Eighteenth-century planting is now past its prime, and the National Trust is replanting. The 2-mile double avenue of common lime is nearly 200 years old and probably passed its best about 180 years ago – it is now an aphid-riddled tunnel, but nice to drive through. Heathy ground at each side can

be driven on to, with forestry conifers beyond. There are odd corners of interest, like an alder coppice just beyond the south end of the avenue, where you cross a bridge. There is some business about charging a heavy parking fee if you approach the Information Centre and shop, by the lake, and presumably it is here you hire your bicycle, paying again: but you can avoid all this. As a drive and a picnic place it is fine: the impressive main entrance gateway sets the tone. The gate is on the A614 (T) near its junction with the A1(T).

Hannah Park Wood, *590 773*, is a 14-acre remnant of Sherwood Forest, with yew, a Woodland Trust property local to Worksop.

Treswell Wood, *761 799*, is an ancient coppice, 119 acres, on clay. A permit and booklet can be got from Mrs E. G. Gilbert, West Croft, Welham, Retford, for 50p.

Alder coppice in Clumber Park

BY THE TRENT

Stapleford Wood, Newark *859 563,* ✦ ,
1100 acres, forest rides, FC
The Forestry Commission, in its crusade to
bring happiness to countless dogs, homeless
lovers and some itinerant woodland
investigators, has really excelled itself in the
parking place to this otherwise functional
forest. The road through the wood is lined
with rhododendron – impressive when in
bloom, but not, I imagine, bringing much joy
to the foresters who find it almost impossible to
remove. The parking place, in the middle of
the forest, is among graceful middle-aged
birches and choice planted trees: planes, a rare
fir, probably Low's fir, and Lawson cypresses
elegantly lopped to about 10 feet up the trunks
– this should be done more often. Instead of
the usual rustic benches there are large blocks
of concrete with lichen growing on them.
There are no organized walks, but miles and
miles of straight rides.

Rhododendron lines the road in Stapleford Wood

Hartsholme *948 697,* ♀ ✦ , *59 acres,*
parkland, CP
There is some woodland around the lake at this
small Country Park 3 miles from the centre of
Lincoln; also fishing, camping and a café.

    Lincoln City's Arboretum is a mature but
fairly ordinary park on the cliffside, with
hospital above and take-away chop suey below.

The Laughton Forest

Laughton Forest: Tuetoes Hills

845 014, ♀, 2000 acres plus, short waymarked walk, FC

Inland sand dunes are the 'hills' of Tuetoes and others among the fertile fields of the Trent alluvial plain: not very noticeable hills, and distinctly dune-shaped. The great wastes of the commons of the tiny villages of Scotter and Laughton now bear a mighty harvest of pines where you could get quite lost – there are nearly 4 square miles of solid trees. The beautiful picnic place is at the northern corner near Susworth, with reassuring glimpses of the flat, arable fields on three sides of a tall stand of pines, where the foresters have even induced some grass to grow. There is a rather tame little walk here, but obviously you can strike out into the depths to the south and east if you take careful note of your route and take a map and compass. Two large meres, one with the pleasant name on the map of Green Howe, now immured in trees, are reputed to harbour unusual water birds; and there are black grouse in the forest. The going is dry but some deep drains are full of mosquitoes. There are some places in England where the straight trunks of pines look absolutely right in the landscape, and this is one of them.

About Hardwick Hill, on the western margins, there is a considerable variety of trees, with poplars and willows. A mile away the cold Trent flows between its lines of cottages like a wide, silent street that no one can cross – there are no ferries now. Instead of the 3-minute crossing you have an hour or so in a bus to get from the east to your neighbour in the west. You can just hear the dull shriek of the M180 to the north, otherwise all is very very quiet: visually relaxing too. I found it rather difficult to drag myself away.

Tuetoes Hills, Laughton Forest

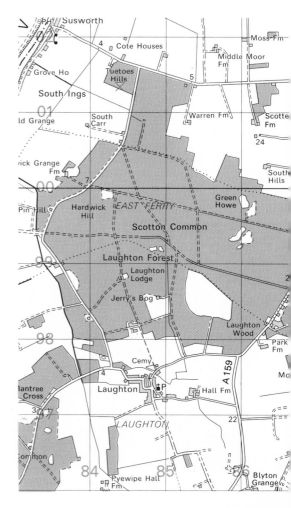

CENTRAL ENGLAND
Lincolnshire: The Wolds

Landranger sheets 121, 122

Woodhall Spa: Kirkby Moor and **Moor Farm** ♀ ♦ ♨, *3½ miles or less, NR*
Ostler's Plantation *215 630,* ♦, *300 acres, several routes, FC*
The two woods are on each side of the road to Kirkby on Bain which leaves the Horncastle road in the suburbs of Woodhall Spa. The Forestry Commission plantation is a massive block, or several blocks, of Scots pine which fit in neatly with the local battery-hen industry.

The small Forestry Commission parking place can be used as the base for a very interesting exploration of oak coppice and birch heath in the nature reserve on the opposite side of the road. There is coppiced rowan too. Birch is cut back to encourage the grass, which is a lovely pink in June. With a wet meadow absolutely full of rushes, cotton-grass and marsh orchid, and drier heath yellow with trefoil, one cannot regret the loss of a few trees. Intermediate stages are retained as well, and the reserve is well looked after. Do not be put off by the small blanket of pine which has been put over the oaks by the road.

The Forestry Commission pinewood offers two walks of 1 mile and 2 miles respectively if you just want to exercise your dog.

At **Martin Moor** a parking place in a pretty birchwood, *217 647,* is on a section of the Viking Way – the Spa Trail – a cinder track on a disused railway with scrub. It would give

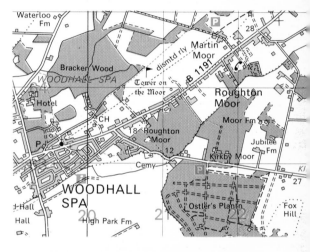

Kirkby Moor: cotton-grass and marsh orchid

most Vikings claustrophobia. A few trees have been planted at the start of the trail: rowans (which are appropriate) and whitebeams (which are not).

Snipe Dales, Winceby *320 683*, ♀ ☙, *2m, dry but uneven, LNR*

This beautifully shaped valley is a nature reserve of the Lincolnshire and South Humberside Trust and is a model of its kind. No apologies for including a non-wooded area.

There are a few scrub trees along the clearly visible spring-line where the valley side cuts into the underlying clay. Trees are being planted and encouraged, the theory being that this was once an oakwood. There is a free leaflet, and there are discreet, beautifully designed and printed information boards. Some old coppiced alders remain at the far end of the walk, with willows under the sheltering wall of a Corsican pine plantation belonging to the Forestry Commission. Fine horsetail, marsh marigold, angelica and marsh thistle grow here. Parking is in a pleasant field where some trees have been planted – including a whitebeam or two.

Other woodlands, such as Dole Wood and Hoplands Wood, in Lincolnshire, can be visited by permit from the Lincolnshire and South Humberside Trust.

Rigsby Wood, Haugh *421 761, ♀,* *37 acres, easy, marked circuit, NR*

Small, but rare, is this ancient ash-oak wood in the lonely fields at the escarpment edge. The reserve is carefully managed and labelled – as one has learnt to expect from the Lincolnshire and South Humberside Trust – and the path is mown: essential this. Much work is being done cutting overgrown ash, and removing dead elm, pine, rabbit wire, etc. It is beautiful too.

Welton (le Marsh) Woods, 4 miles south-east, are known as native oakwood but are marked private except for **Willoughby Wood,** *459 708,* which is a nature reserve. The dirt road leads alongside, to vistas of poplars, fields and other woods, very silent and lonely. The wood itself is an overgrown ash coppice, brooding and dark, and, I will admit, used as I am to woods, scary. I would not care to spend many hours of the night within it – assuming one could penetrate the dense undergrowth.

Gunby Park, *467 669,* National Trust, nearby, is only open on Thursdays. If you feel like a breath of fresh air and can face traversing Skegness, the dunes at **Gibraltar Point,** *556 582,* have scrub of native sea buckthorn – not that it grows high enough to be woodland, but it is an appealing grey shrub with, in winter, silvery spiked twigs and orange-brown berries.

In summer the place is best avoided unless of course you are at the seaside anyway. Gibraltar Point is a National Nature Reserve of 100 acres.

Lindsey is not heavily wooded – it never has been since Domesday, but The Wolds certainly have their charm not least because minor roads are practically deserted. The wide, well-kept verges – most are drove roads and are even called droves in places – have bright green grass glistening with wild flowers, and the wayside trees are large and well formed. There are many new-planted ones as well: sycamore, beech and ash trees, and even some healthy elms. These last are usually hybrid Dutch types, resembling wych elm but more upright in habit and with suckers, absent in pure wych elm, low on the trunk. I did see two or three Plot's elms (*Ulmus carpinifolia* var. *plotii*).

For a tree drive, with fine roadside trees and

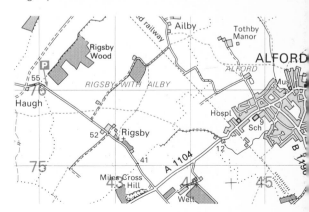

Rigsby Wood at dusk

small woods, from Alford to Louth, turn off the A16(T) to South Ormsby. Turn right after 5 miles to Ruckland and Little Cawthorpe (crossing the A16 at Haugham). Cross the ford in Little Cawthorpe: as you head for Louth you are rewarded by a line of Cornish elms only two of which were dead in 1983. I do wish these dead elms could be cleared, reducing the habitat for the *Scolytus* beetle and probably saving the trees that remain, so long after the height of the epidemic.

Chamber's Plantation, Wragby
148 739, ♀ ♣, 2½m, tiring, FC (Bardney Forest)
This is a special Forestry Commission wood which is managed as a Forest Nature Reserve as well as to produce timber. The smail-leaved lime is much in evidence, but to reach the show-piece, **Hatton Wood**, *163 748*, a mature oak-lime-ash wood, you have what seemed to

me a long walk, probably because much of it is on gravelled forest roads. The margins are decidely interesting and the walk is certainly worth it. This may be the only wood of its kind under proper management, although other woods around do contain oak and lime. Some of the limes are cut, others are standards. The path is well marked and mown and there is no advantage in deviating. There are lots of happy birds and at least one dark red fox: he, or she, didn't seem to see me, but didn't hang about either. Jet planes, no doubt loaded with twice their weight of people-frying devices, exercised at tree-top level, frightening the wits out of the author.

Little Scrubbs Meadow, close by, is a local nature reserve, an old meadow on heavy clay. For this, walk back from the car park by the cottages and take the first woodland track on the right; or follow the Forestry Commission's blue trail, 1 mile. The forestry includes a

Leaves of small-leaved lime

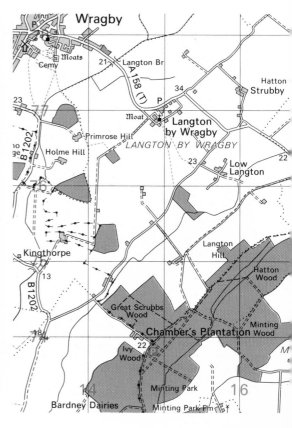

peculiar-looking Scots pine with very shaggy bark – not a native strain I guess – Japanese cedar, and a small-leaved spruce which could almost be the oriental spruce; but not quite – it is the Christmas tree or Norway spruce but again a peculiar strain, or maybe poor growth.

Willingham Woods, Market Rasen
139 885, ✦, *1m and 3m walks, FC*
A large picnic place on the main road has space for ball games and a pull-in for lorries. There are some ponds. This a large forest of pines, strong on geometry. Much quieter is a nature reserve at **Linwood Warren** to the south, opposite the golf course: some oak–birch woodland (with lily of the valley) around an open heath, *133 877*. You can also walk along the margins of the Forestry Commission's spruce woods which adjoin. Some of the spruce, as well as some of the pine, is spreading onto the heath grassland, which surely should

not be allowed. The grass is a beautiful pink in June, but I could find no flowers, only leaves, of the lily of the valley. It is said to be decreasing everywhere. Other wild flowers were abundant. I did not find the round-leaved sundew, probably because I kept to the footpath, as directed by the *Nature Reserves Handbook*, 1982. According to the *Guide to Britain's Nature Reserves*, 1984, I should not even have been there without a permit. Both books are published by the Royal Society for Nature Conservation, and I think it is time they made up their minds about permits, or the system will be 'brought into disrepute'.

I did stray into the small birch and oak woodland. Here I did not see, nor did I expect to see, the badger, red squirrel, or the water shrew. If you do wait long enough to see any wild life you will be bitten to death by the gnats or mosquitoes which breed in the woodland ditches.

The path though Hatton Wood: oak and lime

Index